KINGDOM SOLDIERS

ADVANCING THE KINGDOM OF GOD

RICHARD "CUZZ" ROBINSON

ISBN (eBook): 978-1-967120-33-8

ISBN (Paperback): 978-1-967120-34-5

Library of Congress Control Number: 2026902256

Cover design by Steve Oros.

Published by Indie Christian Book in Bloomington, Illinois, U.S.A.

CONTENTS

FOREWORD

JEFF B. MILLER

I'll never forget it. I was scared. Exhausted. Homesick already. The one thought going through my mind was, "What have I done?" These were my feelings five minutes into my first night of Basic Military Training in the U.S. Air Force.

Reading Richard's book, I can't help but remember those first days in the military. They took our clothes, they cut our hair off, they gave us uniforms, a new code, a new allegiance, a new brotherhood. They gave us a new identity as airmen training to defend America and fight for her causes.

I remember all of that reading the book in your hands, because Pastor Richard Robinson does a masterful job of relating the Christian life to the life of a soldier. The Bible says,

You then, my child, be strengthened by the grace that is in Christ Jesus, and what you have heard from me in the presence of many witnesses entrust to faithful men, who will be able to teach others also. Share in suffering as a good soldier of Christ Jesus. No soldier gets entangled in civilian pursuits, since his aim is to please the one who enlisted him.

— 2 TIMOTHY 2:1-4

God says a lot of things about us in His Word. We are His children, His sons and daughters, His flock, even His bondservants, but Richard draws our attention to one very important aspect of our identity as the family God. We are called to be soldiers. We are called to serve and protect His Kingdom and advance it against the enemy of our souls as our great Commander and High Priest takes back territory and spreads His glorious Kingdom of Light over the dominion of darkness and evil.

It is true that humanity has suffered under the one who staged a coup in the garden of Eden and brought sin, suffering, and death on God's creation (Genesis 3). It is also true that Christ, our Commander, was always the Lamb slain since the foundation of the world who would come and conquer by coming and dying on the cross for us. The Word says that His cross secured the victory and made us alive.

Colossians 2:13-15 says,

> And you, who were dead in your trespasses and the uncircumcision of your flesh, God made alive together with him, having forgiven us all our trespasses, by canceling the record of debt that stood against us with its legal demands. This he set aside, nailing it to the cross. *He disarmed the rulers and authorities and put them to open shame, by triumphing over them in him.* (Emphasis added)

But that was D-Day. Now we approach V-Day as the Army of Heaven. We've been commissioned and called to, as my brother will say, "leave the trenches" and get into the battle.

Read this book if you want to be informed and inspired.

Read it if you want to take your place in God's Army as a Kingdom Soldier, advancing the glorious Kingdom of our glorious King! It's a field manual and an inspiration. This is your first step to becoming what God's called you to be.

INTRODUCTION

Have you ever assembled a puzzle with a few thousand pieces, placed the last piece, and then realized one is missing? That one missing piece can drain all the air out of you. You might tell yourself, "It's just one piece." But the truth is, that missing piece keeps you from enjoying the 1,999 pieces that fit perfectly together.

In this book, I want you to understand something clearly. You are not insignificant. You are not extra. You are not a leftover piece on the table. You are a needed and valuable part of God's Kingdom agenda in the world.

God said it this way: "For I know the plans I have for you," declares the Lord, "plans to prosper you and not to harm you, plans to give you hope and a future" (Jeremiah 29:11). That verse is not sentimental. It is a declaration of God's intentionality. In His sovereignty, His supreme power and authority, God established a plan for the advancement of His Kingdom that includes you. That is why you cannot afford to diminish your place in the Kingdom of God. The Lord did not make a mistake when He formed you, saved you, and positioned you. He recognizes your value, even when you struggle to see it.

This is tied directly to what happened in your born-again experience. Salvation did not simply change your destination. It changed your identity. Something happened in your spirit. You were made new, connected to Him, and commissioned for purpose.

Scripture says, "As He is, so are we in this world" (1 John 4:17). That statement is not meant to inflate your ego. It is meant to anchor your confidence. It means you are not trying to represent Christ from the sidelines. You are meant to live connected to Him, carrying His life, His nature, and His authority into the world.

That is why it matters that you see yourself the way God sees you. "I will praise thee; for I am fearfully and wonderfully made" (Psalm 139:14). If you cannot see your value, you will do what the man in Matthew 25 did in the parable of the talents. You will bury what God entrusted to you, not because you are lazy, but because you do not recognize the worth of what you carry. Even though you are one person, you are significant. You matter.

You are not here by accident, and you were never meant to sit on the sidelines or live in the trenches.

God has called every believer to be a Kingdom Soldier. That means you have been entrusted with divine purpose.

So what is a Kingdom Soldier?

A Kingdom Soldier is a believer who aligns with the Kingdom of God and lives with a clear aim: to serve under God's rule and bring the government of heaven to bear on earth. A Kingdom Soldier understands the influence and empowerment of the Holy Spirit. He is the Spirit of Truth. He guides. He gives wisdom. He navigates your life so that what you do is not merely human effort, but God working through you.

Heaven runs on a different system than earth.

God's way is often the opposite of what the world applauds.

That is why embracing your role, even when it feels small, carries eternal weight. The Holy Spirit uniquely chose you and your assignment to bring glory to God and influence lives.

Jesus' mission was to bring the Kingdom of Heaven to earth. His teachings and actions continually pointed people toward that reality. When the disciples asked Him how to pray, He began with Kingdom alignment: "Thy kingdom come, Thy will be done in earth, as it is in heaven" (Matthew 6:9–10). That prayer is not religious poetry. It is a battle cry. It is the believer asking for heaven's rule to be expressed in real life.

To fulfill your assignment as a Kingdom Soldier, you need to understand what a kingdom is. Dr. Myles Munroe put it plainly:

> The Kingdom of God is not merely religion, but the governing influence of a King over His territory. It is God's will, purpose, and intent expressed in a way that creates culture and reflects His nature. It is not only a future destination. It is a present reality to be experienced now through faith, obedience, and seeking God's righteousness. In other words, God's Kingdom is God's rule, made visible through God's people.*

THE KINGDOM OF GOD

The Kingdom of God is the government of God ruling over earthly affairs. That is why entry requires being born again. God is Spirit, and the Kingdom is spiritual. Heaven comes to earth when God's ways, thoughts, and actions are expressed through our lives. When we develop a passion for His Kingdom, His divine order is restored in the places we live and serve. That passion brings revelation. It clarifies purpose. It

---

* Dr. Myles Munroe. *Kingdom Principles: Preparing for Kingdom Experience and Expansion*, Destiny Image Publishers, 2009, pg. 31.

strengthens assignment. Scripture tells us to seek His Kingdom first, because it is the doorway into God's heart (Matthew 6:33).

The Kingdom is not a physical territory and not limited to geography. It is a spiritual reality with earthly impact. However, even a spiritual kingdom must have four essential elements:

- A King (ruler)
- Territory (place)
- Citizens (subject)
- Laws (rules)

To "seek" is to try to find or discover by searching or questioning. When we played "hide and seek" as a kid, we looked behind trees, cars, or any place we thought a person would hide. When we are told to "seek first the kingdom of God" (Matthew 6:33), it must be our chief priority, something that we diligently pursue because we want to understand it.

> The greatest secret to living effectively on earth is understanding the principle and power of priorities. Our life is the sum total of all the decisions we make every day, and those decisions are determined by our priorities.*

It is hard to operate in God's Kingdom if we don't understand it and make it a priority. Our identity and purpose is wrapped up in understanding the Kingdom.

We are told also to seek His righteousness, a word that implies right positioning or alignment. We take our car to the auto shop when we feel it pulling to the side or notice uneven wear as a result of hitting potholes. As believers, we must align ourselves with the heart of God in order to live and operate

---

* Dr. Myles Munroe. *Kingdom Principles: Preparing for Kingdom Experience and Expansion*, Destiny Image Publishers, 2009, pg. 24.

effectively in His Kingdom. Our righteousness is not the result of our efforts but is because of the righteousness of our Lord.

> In essence, righteousness describes the maintenance of the rightly aligned relationship with a governing authority so as to qualify for the right to receive governmental privileges.*

A DIVINE ASSIGNMENT

In January 2013, after pastoring for eleven years, I received another assignment from the Lord.

I want to be transparent. My new assignment was a result of me throwing in the towel after experiencing much frustration and disappointment. The Lord knew that I wanted to become what I call a spiritual bodybuilder for the Kingdom of God. I wanted to strengthen believers for growth, clarity, and assignment. I also wanted to continue conducting evangelism and discipleship workshops, helping believers share the Gospel effectively on a larger scale. This is something I have done for more than thirty-five years, and I believe it is my assignment from the Father.

Sadly, I have seen how many Christians do not know how to share the Gospel clearly. Many do not understand the basic tenets of their faith, what they believe and why. That is a serious gap, because Kingdom Soldiers are meant to be equipped and armed, not only to endure, but to reach the lost.

Think about how the world trains for what matters to them. Athletes prepare for a season with rigorous discipline. Many invest thousands of dollars in trainers and nutritionists because they want to develop their craft. Our government sends recruits through basic training at enormous cost because it understands

---

* Dr. Myles Munroe. *Kingdom Principles: Preparing for Kingdom Experience and Expansion*, Destiny Image Publishers, 2009, pg. 91.

something simple: You do not send untrained people into conflict.

So why do we often send new believers into spiritual battle without spiritual training or training in evangelism?

Jesus said, "The harvest truly is plenteous, but the labourers are few" (Matthew 9:37 KJV). A farmer who fails to harvest suffers loss. Crops decay. Pest problems multiply. Future income is damaged. And if missed harvest carries consequences in a field, what happens when we miss opportunities to share the Gospel with a family member, a friend, or a stranger?

This is a body ministry. It is shared work. Paul said, "I have planted, Apollos watered; but God gave the increase" (1 Corinthians 3:6–7 KJV). We do our part, and God does what only God can do.

God is love, and He proved it by sending His Son. That means we must remember what we are: His representatives. Scripture says we have been given the ministry of reconciliation, and that we are ambassadors for Christ, with God making His appeal through us (2 Corinthians 5:18–20). That is not reserved for the "special few." That is the calling of every believer.

Whether we like it or not, we are in a spiritual battle. That reality should not make us fearful. It should make us focused. God's desire is that none perish but that all come to repentance (2 Peter 3:9). People's eternal futures are at stake. That is why we must prioritize what matters.

Jesus was not only our Lord and Savior. He is the ultimate Kingdom Soldier. His earthly life reflected the Father. He defeated the devil. He conquered sin, death, hell, sickness, and the grave. His victory is why we serve from a position of victory. We do not fear the enemy, because our Commander-in-Chief has already conquered him at the cross. The resurrection sealed the victory. That is why Scripture says we are more than conquerors (Romans 8:37).

Unlike elite military forces trained with physical weapons, the Kingdom Soldier belongs to an elite force of a different kind: the army of the living God. Our weapons are not carnal. They are spiritual. God has issued us the armor of God: the belt of truth; the breastplate of righteousness; the shoes of the Gospel of peace; the shield of faith; the helmet of salvation; the sword of the Spirit, which is the Word of God; and prayer, which accesses God's power and guidance. The believer's daily bread is the Word, our manual for living, standing, and resisting evil within and without.

This book is for those who sense there is more to their faith than attendance and survival. It is for those who feel a tug in their spirit and want to make an impact and leave a legacy that outlives them. It is for those who are tired of sitting on the sidelines and living in the trenches but do not know how to engage. My prayer is that by the end of this book, you move from passive Christianity into purposeful Kingdom service, with clarity about your assignment and confidence in how to carry it out.

Too many believers continue to live from the trenches and the sidelines. In World War I, trenches were defensive structures, not permanent homes. They provided temporary cover, a place for planning, and protection from incoming fire. They were meant to serve a purpose, then be left behind.

The days of living in trenches are over. The Lord is calling believers to the front lines, not in arrogance, but in obedience. When Christians live as if the trenches are home, they miss the chance to help effect change in someone else's life. The Lord is making a clarion call in this hour. He is raising up believers who are bold, compassionate, rooted in faith, committed to the Word, and able to explain what they believe and why. He is calling those who have been inactive to come off the sidelines and engage in the advancement of His Kingdom.

You do not have to be wealthy, educated, or impressive. But you must be willing.

In my years of ministry, I have spoken with many who felt they did not matter to God. Even after being born again, they kept rehearsing the enemy's lies: "God hasn't forgiven you. Look at all the people you've hurt." Those mind games have trapped many believers in shame. And in a world where so many struggle with low self-esteem, depression, identity confusion, PTSD, and other mental health battles, the need for trained Kingdom Soldiers has never been greater. People are hurting. And God intends to send help through His people.

By the end of this book, you will no longer underestimate the power of your obedience, the importance of your role, or the weight of your influence in the advancement of God's Kingdom. You will receive training in how to share the Gospel and how to live as someone armed and trained. God can create the toughest soldiers through the hardest battles, and He can use a yielded vessel in ways you cannot yet imagine.

As you read, remember how great our God is. Isaiah says, "Lift up your eyes on high and see: who created these...because he is strong in power, not one is missing" (Isaiah 40:25–26). If God calls the stars by name and not one is missing, you can be sure He knows your name and your place in His plan.

Our Father is sovereign. He spoke the universe into being. And the key to our effectiveness as Kingdom Soldiers is remembering that He is the source of our wisdom and strength. Jesus said, "I am the vine, ye are the branches...for without me ye can do nothing" (John 15:5 KJV). As long as we stay connected to Him, interwoven in Him, we will bear fruit.

For we are his workmanship, created in Christ Jesus for good

works, which God prepared beforehand, that we should walk
in them.

— EPHESIANS 2:10

And that brings us back to the puzzle.

You are not the piece nobody needs. You are not the piece
that does not matter.

You are the piece God prepared in advance.

And it is time to take your place.

PREFACE

I never had the honor of serving in the military, but I want to honor all those who are currently serving and the millions who have served. As I write this book, I do feel a sense of inadequacy due to not having had the opportunity to serve. However, as a Kingdom Soldier, I am an agent of the Living God, and I answer to the greatest Commander in Chief ever. I have been under His command for almost fifty years. During that time, I have gone AWOL, abandoned my post, and was a POW of the bad choices that I made. But I've also been through my own spiritual bootcamp, technical school, and specialized training.

Over the years, so many brave soldiers have been recognized for their bravery and sacrifices, with many receiving various awards, such as the Medal of Honor, the Distinguished Service Cross, the Navy Cross, the Air Force Cross, the Silver Star, the Bronze Star, the Purple Heart, etc. This is just a partial list of awards given to our brave men and women for their services and sacrifices.

However, the title of greatest Soldier and the most distinguished honor of all time hands down must go to Jesus Christ, the conqueror of death, hell and the grave, and the Redeemer of our Fallen Soul. Even greater than Alexander the Great, Genghis Khan, Leonidas I, Hannibal, Shaka Zulu, Attila the Hun, Julius Caesar, Spartacus, Sun Tzu, etc. Their accomplishments and achievements are no match to our Lord.

His military credentials would read:

Unmatched strategic leadership: Non-confrontational campaign.

Established a Kingdom without borders: Not limited by geography.

Recruitment: Troops not trained in combat, but in humble service.

Perfect obedience to the Commander: His Heavenly Father.

Endured maximum hardship: The Cross, the greatest act of courage.

Love for the enemy: His love showed the power of His Kingdom.

Conquered death itself: The resurrection, His ultimate victory. His soldiers need not Fear Death.

Seated as the eternal King: His ascension to heaven confirms His permanent reign.

The final promotion: The Kingdom Soldier will join the resurrected King for all eternity.

Has influenced more lives than any other, living or dead.

PART I

THE CALL TO ARMS

1

THE SLEEPING GIANT

I grew up in church. That statement might sound like the beginning of a testimony about deep spiritual roots and early faith formation. But for me, it was something far more complicated. My sisters and I were in Sunday School and Worship Service every single week without exception. Our family was known in the congregation. People greeted us by name. They watched us grow up year after year. We were fixtures in that community, as reliable as the oak pews and the hymnals in the racks.

I was the only boy out of six children, and because of that, I was often given privileges that my sisters were not afforded. People made a fuss over me in ways they did not make over the girls. I received attention and exceptions that, looking back, I did not deserve and certainly did not earn. Those privileges might have been harmless when I was a child, when they amounted to extra dessert or getting to sit in the front seat of the car. But as I got older, those same patterns of special treatment became excuses. They became reasons to believe that the rules applied differently to me than to everyone else.

By the time I reached my junior and senior years of high

school, I had begun to slip in ways that were visible to anyone paying attention. The late nights with my girlfriend and my friends made Sunday mornings increasingly difficult. My body was tired from staying out too late on Saturday nights, and my spirit was even more fatigued from the double life I was living. I still went to church occasionally, but not with any consistency. The weekly rhythm that had defined my childhood became sporadic and half-hearted. I showed up when it was convenient, when I was not too tired, when I did not have something more appealing to do.

Even so, I held tightly to one comfortable belief that allowed me to continue without too much guilt. As long as I made it to church on Sunday morning, I believed I was Heaven bound. It did not matter what I did the other six days of the week. It did not matter how I lived when no one from church was watching. It did not matter that my heart was far from God even when my body was sitting in His house. I had reduced salvation to attendance and attendance eventually to occasional appearance. That distortion of the Gospel gave me just enough religious cover to quiet my conscience without requiring any real change.

What made it even easier to believe this lie was watching the adults in the church whose lifestyles clearly did not line up with what Scripture taught. I saw men who led prayers on Sunday and led very different lives on Monday. I saw women who sang in the choir and spread gossip in the parking lot. I saw families that looked picture-perfect during the service and fell apart behind closed doors. If they could live such inconsistent lives and still feel spiritually secure, then why could I not do the same? Their hypocrisy gave me permission for my own. Their compromise became my justification. I looked at them and concluded that this must be how Christianity worked. You showed up. You went through the motions. You maintained appearances. And somehow, that was enough.

But deep down, in the quiet places where I could not hide from myself, I knew better.

I knew right from wrong. My mother had taught me well. The Scriptures I had heard since childhood had planted seeds of truth that I could not entirely uproot, no matter how hard I tried to ignore them.

I knew what the Bible said. I sat through countless sermons and Sunday School lessons. The words were stored somewhere in my memory, even if I was not living by them.

I knew my obedience was selective. I obeyed the parts that were easy or convenient. I ignored the parts that would have required sacrifice or change. I picked and chose from God's commands like items on a buffet, taking what appealed to me and leaving the rest untouched.

And even though I did not say it out loud to anyone, even though I maintained my external image as a young man from a good church family, I knew I was drifting. I could feel the distance growing between who I pretended to be and who I actually was. I could sense the emptiness expanding in my soul, even as I filled my life with distractions and pleasures. I was moving away from God, and some part of me knew it, even while another part of me refused to acknowledge it.

SELECTIVE OBEDIENCE AND A GROWING VOID

Selective obedience has a way of creating a spiritual void that grows larger over time. You try to ignore it, but it nags at you in quiet moments. You attempt to fill it with entertainment, relationships, achievements, and distractions, but nothing quite fits the shape of the hole. You rationalize your behavior with arguments that sound reasonable in your own ears. You justify your choices by pointing to others who seem to be doing worse. You excuse your compromise by reminding yourself of the ways you are still better than many people you know. But through all the rationalizing and justifying and excusing, the truth remains in the back of your mind like a splinter you cannot remove.

I had become a hearer of the Word but not a doer. James warned against this very condition in his letter, comparing such a person to someone who looks in a mirror and immediately forgets what they look like. That was me precisely. I heard sermons that convicted me on Sunday and forgot them by Monday. I listened to truth without letting it transform me. I received the Word without responding to it.

I was slowly becoming what I would later come to call a *pew sitter*: someone present in body but absent in heart. Someone who occupies space in the sanctuary without occupying their place in the Kingdom. Someone who checks the religious box without checking their own soul. My attendance record might have looked acceptable on paper, but my spiritual condition was deteriorating beneath the surface.

I did not see it then, at least not clearly. That is the nature of spiritual sleep. When you are asleep, you do not know you are asleep. You have no awareness of your unconscious state. You dream, and the dreams feel real. You rest in false comfort, unaware that dangers surround you. The sleeping person does not recognize their vulnerability until something or someone wakes them.

I needed to be awakened. But I did not know how to wake myself, and I was not even certain that I wanted to be awakened. The sleep was comfortable in its own way. The dreams I had constructed for my life felt pleasant enough. Why would I want to be disturbed?

THE PASSIVE CHURCH I LATER SAW EVERYWHERE

Years later, after I had answered God's call to ministry and eventually became a senior pastor myself, I began to recognize in others the same condition God had delivered me from. What I had experienced as a young man was not unique to me. It was an epidemic affecting churches all across the country. Everywhere I looked, I found people who attended faithfully but remained spiritually inactive. They filled the pews on Sunday mornings but seemed absent from the mission every other day of the week.

The more I observed and the more I pastored, the more I began to identify several categories of Christians who reflected what I had once been. These categories emerged from years of watching, counseling, preaching, and praying. They are not meant to be harsh labels hurled at struggling believers. They are meant to be honest descriptions that help people recognize where they might be stuck.

One of these labels I already mentioned, *pew sitters*. These are people who attend services regularly, sometimes for years or even decades, but never participate in any form of ministry. They arrive, they sit, they listen, they leave. They are consumers of religious services rather than contributors to the Kingdom. They receive, but they do not give. They absorb, but they do not act. If you asked them to serve in any capacity, they would have a ready excuse for why they cannot. They treat church as something that happens to them rather than something they are part of building.

Then there are the *pew warmers*. These believers look devoted on Sundays. They sing the songs with apparent enthusiasm. They take notes during the sermon. They greet others warmly in the lobby. They may even serve occasionally when asked. But their lives during the week tell a different story. They live disconnected from the faith they profess. Their Monday through Saturday existence bears little resemblance to their Sunday performance. They are not actively pursuing wickedness, necessarily, but neither are they actively pursuing Christ. They are inconsistent in ways that leave them vulnerable and ineffective.

The *pew potatoes* are passive observers who view church primarily as entertainment rather than engagement. They come to watch rather than worship. They come to be impressed rather than transformed. They evaluate services the way they might evaluate a movie or a concert, giving mental reviews based on whether the music was good enough or the sermon was interesting enough to hold their attention. Church exists to serve their preferences. If it fails to meet their expectations, they will shop around for something more appealing. The thought that they might be called to serve rather than be served rarely crosses their minds.

Passive Christians are individuals who hear God's Word week after week but never act on what they hear. They accumulate spiritual knowledge without ever applying it. They could quote Scripture and explain doctrine, but their lives do not reflect the truths they claim to believe. They are hearers but not doers, exactly as James warned against. The Word enters their ears but never reaches their hands and feet.

Finally, there are the *inactive members*. These are people whose names appear on the church roster but who have no real presence in the church's life. They joined at some point, perhaps years ago, and they are still counted among the membership, but they have functionally disappeared. They do not attend regularly. They do not serve in any capacity. They do not give financially. They do not participate in fellowship or discipleship. They are members in name only, carrying a label without embodying its meaning.

These categories are not designed to condemn anyone. I

was every one of these things at different points in my journey. I know the condition from the inside. These descriptions are meant to diagnose rather than judge. Because you cannot fix what you will not face. You cannot address a problem you refuse to acknowledge. Honest assessment is the first step toward genuine change.

And spiritually passive Christians are vulnerable in ways they often fail to recognize. Peter warned that the devil prowls around like a roaring lion, seeking someone to devour. Lions do not attack the strong and vigilant members of the herd. Lions target the weak, the isolated, the distracted, the unaware. The devil operates the same way. He looks for believers who have let down their guard, who have drifted from community, who have grown passive in their faith.

The Old Testament tells us that when Amalek attacked the people of Israel in the wilderness, he struck the rear ranks first. He targeted the faint and the weary and the stragglers who could not keep up with the main body of the people. That is exactly who the enemy still targets today. He goes after those who have fallen behind, those who have grown tired, those who are not keeping pace with what God is doing.

Many believers who sit but do not serve eventually drift into discouragement, confusion, and spiritual boredom. Church becomes a routine they maintain rather than a calling they pursue. What once felt meaningful becomes mechanical. What once stirred their hearts becomes familiar and flat. They become spiritually stagnant, like a pond with no outlet. The water stops flowing, and eventually it begins to grow foul.

I saw this pattern repeated over and over during my years as a pastor. Good-hearted people with no apparent desire to step into their calling. Churches filled with members who loved the fellowship and enjoyed the friendships but avoided any real responsibility. A few faithful volunteers doing the work of many while the majority spectated from a comfortable distance. The same faces showing up for service projects again and again while most of the congregation remained absent.

Awakening is not just about coming alive per se. This is not the Church that Jesus envisioned when He spoke of building something the gates of hell could not prevail against. He never called us to be spectators who watch from the stands while others do the work. He called us to be soldiers who engage in the battle. He never called us to be consumers who evaluate religious experiences based on our preferences. He called us to be servants who lay down our lives for others.

The Church was never meant to be a gathering of passive observers. It was meant to be an army of active participants. And awakening is the process by which spectators become soldiers.

THE ROUND TABLE VISION OF THE CHURCH

One of my favorite pictures of what Christian community could look like comes from the legends of King Arthur and his Round Table. There were no high seats or low seats at that table. No corners where the powerful could distance themselves from the common. Each knight sat shoulder to shoulder with the others, equal in honor and unified in purpose. Rank and wealth and background faded into irrelevance when they gathered as brothers under one king.

And before they rode into battle, they would place their swords together at the center of the table, symbolizing their unity under their one shared sovereign. They were different men with different gifts and different backgrounds, but they served the same lord and fought for the same cause. That act of laying down their individual weapons and combining them into one represented something profound about what it means to be part of something larger than yourself.

That is how the Church is supposed to function.

One King at the center of everything. Jesus Christ, the risen Lord, the head of the body, the one to whom all authority has been given. Not a pastor or a bishop or a denomination or a tradition. Christ alone.

One mission that unites us across every division that might otherwise separate us. The Great Commission, given by Jesus, to make disciples of all nations. Not our individual agendas or our personal preferences or our cultural assumptions. His mission.

One body composed of many members who each contribute what they have been given. Not competition between parts. Not comparison that produces envy or pride. Cooperation toward a shared goal.

One purpose that gives meaning to everything we do. The glory of God and the advance of His Kingdom. Not our own glory. Not our own kingdoms. His.

When Christ is truly at the center, ego dies. You stop asking how you can be recognized and start asking how you can be useful. Comparison dies. You stop measuring yourself against others and start measuring yourself against your own calling. Competition dies. You stop viewing other believers as rivals only, as wonderful as the individual Christian experience is. It is about finding your place in the family of God. It is about discovering where you fit in the body of Christ. It is about standing shoulder to shoulder with other believers, each contributing your unique gifts and abilities, ready to serve your King in whatever way He directs.

The sleeping giant does not merely need to wake up as an individual. The sleeping giant needs to take its place among other awakened believers who together form something far more powerful than any of them could be alone.

2

MY FIRST WEEKEND AT ISU

I n the fall of 1974, I arrived at Illinois State University filled with excitement about the independence that awaited me. For the first time in my life, there would be no curfew imposed by parents. There would be no one checking to make sure I was home at a reasonable hour. There would be no authority figures looking over my shoulder and monitoring my choices. Freedom stretched before me like an open highway, and I was eager to drive as fast as I wanted.

My cousin Denzil and I were best friends, and we had made arrangements to be roommates in the dormitory. We had grown up together, gotten into trouble together, and now we would experience college together. We were ready to enjoy everything university life had to offer. Our plans did not include much room for church or spiritual matters. We were young men ready to explore the world on our own terms.

But God had another plan entirely. His plans rarely align with our plans, and His timing rarely matches our expectations. He was about to interrupt our agenda with His own.

That first Sunday on campus, something prompted us to attend a church service. I am not entirely sure why we went.

Perhaps it was habit ingrained from childhood. Perhaps it was a lingering sense of obligation that we had not yet fully shaken off. Perhaps it was the quiet whisper of the Holy Spirit beginning His work in ways we did not recognize. Whatever the reason, Denzil and I found ourselves walking toward a campus church service that would change the trajectory of my entire life.

I expected something quiet and traditional, similar to the churches I had known growing up. I expected orderly hymns sung from hymnals. I expected a predictable order of service with familiar rhythms. I expected polite religion practiced by polite people in polite ways. I expected to check the church box for the week and then get on with the business of enjoying my newfound freedom.

What I walked into stunned me completely.

The place was filled with college students my own age. Not elderly members who had been attending for decades. Not middle-aged parents dragging reluctant children. Students like me. Young people who had chosen to be there, who wanted to be there, who seemed genuinely glad to be there.

The music was loud, joyful, and passionate in ways I had never experienced in a church setting. It was not the solemn hymns I knew. It was praise that seemed to burst from hearts that could not contain it. Young people were worshiping God with their whole beings. They were shouting praises. They were dancing in the aisles. They were speaking in tongues and lifting their hands toward heaven as if reaching for Someone they actually believed was present.

Then they began giving testimonies, standing before the congregation to share how God had helped them during the week. They talked about everything from unexpected grant money arriving just when tuition was due to God providing food when their cupboards were empty. They shared stories of answered prayers and divine interventions and miraculous provisions. They spoke of God as if He were actively involved in the details of their daily lives, as if they had ongoing conversations with Him, as if they actually knew Him personally.

It was not the noise that shocked me, though there was plenty of noise, and it was certainly different from anything I had experienced.

It was their sincerity.

It was their gratitude.

It was their genuine relationship with God.

These were not people going through religious motions. These were not performers putting on a show for an audience. These were young men and women who had encountered something real, and their lives had been transformed by that encounter. Their worship was not performance. It was response. Their testimonies were not rehearsed speeches. They were authentic reports from people who had actually experienced what they described.

And their authenticity exposed something in me that I had managed to ignore for years.

I did not have what they had. I did not know God the way they knew Him. I had grown up in church, but I had never encountered the living Christ in a way that transformed how I lived. I had religion without relationship. I had knowledge without intimacy. I had the external trappings of faith without the internal reality.

When I heard them talk about being saved, about enjoying fellowship with God, about having a real relationship with Jesus Christ, it hit me with devastating clarity: I had been in church all my life, and I had missed the very heart of what Christianity was supposed to be. I had confused familiarity with family. I had mistaken attendance for belonging. I had assumed that growing up around Christians made me a Christian, *just as growing up in a garage might make someone assume they were a car.*

That realization shook me to my core. It disturbed me in a way I could not shake off when the service ended. I could not dismiss what I had witnessed as emotionalism or charismatic excess. Something was different about these people, and I knew it. They possessed something I did not have, and I could no longer pretend otherwise.

SPIRITUAL AWAKENING BEGINS

Denzil and I kept returning to those services. We could not stay away. Week after week, we found ourselves drawn back to that campus church where we had stumbled upon something our souls desperately needed. We attended the Sunday worship services, with their passionate praise and powerful testimonies. We joined the midweek Bible studies, where the Scriptures were taught with clarity and applied with conviction. We were hungry for what we were seeing, and we kept coming back for more.

Slowly, sometimes painfully, God began breaking down my excuses. Every justification I had constructed over the years came under His examination. Every rationalization I had used to avoid surrender was exposed for the flimsy defense it truly was. He peeled back layers of self-deception that I had not even recognized as deception. He showed me how far I had drifted from the truth while convincing myself I was still close enough.

He exposed the emptiness of my casual church life. What I had considered normal Christianity was revealed as sub-Christianity. What I had accepted as adequate was shown to be woefully insufficient. The life I had been living as a church-going young man who occasionally showed up on Sundays was not the life Jesus had called His followers to live. It was a pale imitation, a shadow without substance, a form without power.

He opened my eyes to see the truth I had been avoiding. I was spiritually asleep. I had been asleep for years, perhaps my entire life. I had never truly been awake to the reality of God and His claim on my life. I had existed in a fog of religious familiarity that kept me from seeing clearly. And now, for the first time, I was beginning to wake up.

Over the next year and a half, God continued His awakening work in both me and Denzil. He stirred something in our hearts that we could no longer ignore, no matter how much our old selves might have preferred to stay comfortable. The hunger He had placed in us demanded to be satisfied. The conviction He had planted in us refused to be silenced. The truth He had revealed to us could not be unseen.

Eventually, we both surrendered our lives fully to Jesus Christ. Not the partial surrender I had practiced before, where I gave God access to certain areas while keeping others locked away for myself. Full surrender. Complete surrender. The kind of surrender that holds nothing back and makes no exceptions.

And once God woke me up, I knew I could not go back to selective obedience. Something real had begun in my life. Something irreversible. Something that would shape everything that followed.

What I discovered during that season at ISU became the foundation of this entire book. It is a truth that many churchgoers need to hear and few want to admit: It is possible to be raised in church and still be spiritually asleep. Church attendance does not equal spiritual life. Religious familiarity does not equal personal faith. Growing up around believers does not automatically make you a believer any more than growing up in a library makes you a scholar.

God had to wake me up. He had to interrupt my comfortable sleep with His disturbing truth. He had to shine light into the darkness I had grown accustomed to. And as I would later learn, He was not only awakening me. He was preparing me for something I could not have imagined. The awakening was just the beginning. What came next would give that awakening purpose and direction.

A CLARION CALL YOU CANNOT IGNORE

When God awakened me at ISU, He did more than stir my emotions. He did more than make me feel spiritual for a season. Awakening shines a light on where you are. It reveals the truth about your condition. But calling is something different. Calling reveals where you are meant to go. It points you toward a destination and gives your life a trajectory.

From the earliest days of my Christian walk, I sensed something unmistakable rising in my spirit. God was issuing a clarion call. Not just to pastors. Not just to evangelists. Not just to the spiritually polished or the naturally bold. This call went out to every believer who claimed the name of Christ.

A clarion call is not vague. It is sharp and unmistakable. In ancient Israel and throughout the Roman world, trumpets signaled commands that could not be misunderstood. One sound meant attack. Another meant retreat. Another meant march. Another meant stand still and hold your position. A confused sound put soldiers in danger. A clear sound saved lives and won battles.

That is how the Great Commission began to feel in my spirit. It was not a gentle suggestion whispered in passing. It was a command issued with authority and urgency.

Jesus did not whisper when He gave His final instructions to His disciples. He proclaimed with the full weight of His resurrected authority, "Go and make disciples of all nations." This was not a suggestion for the spiritually bold or the naturally outgoing. This was not an invitation extended only to those with seminary degrees or missionary callings. This was a command for every believer who had experienced the saving grace of Jesus Christ.

From that moment forward, I knew I could not be a Christian in name only. I could not sit in pews and collect sermons like souvenirs. I could not treat my faith as a private matter between me and God while the world around me perished without hope. If I was going to grow, I had to move. I had to obey. I had to become spiritually ready and spiritually available for whatever assignments God placed before me.

Awakening reveals the need. Calling reveals the next step. And once you hear the call, you cannot pretend you did not hear it. You can only choose whether to obey or to ignore. This was the beginning of my training. This was where the real work of discipleship began.

GROWING MY SPIRITUAL MUSCLES

Competition has always been in my blood. Even as a young boy, I liked winning spelling bees. I liked succeeding in sports. I liked rising to a challenge and proving that I could accomplish what others doubted. That competitive drive did not disappear when I became a Christian. In fact, salvation intensified it and gave it new direction.

I wanted to grow in my faith with the same intensity I had applied to athletics and academics. I wanted to learn the Scriptures with depth and precision. I wanted to be useful to God in tangible ways. I did not want to be a spectator in the Kingdom. I wanted to be a participant.

So I began memorizing Scripture with purpose. Not random verses that sounded nice. Soul-winning verses. Verses that taught me who I was in Christ and what I was called to do. I memorized the Romans Road and the key passages that explained the Gospel clearly. I studied the words of Jesus until they became part of my thinking. I filled my mind with truth so that when opportunities arose, I would have something of substance to offer.

Before long, I joined our campus outreach ministry, called F.A.T., which stood for Faith Action Team. My brother Michael led the ministry, and he could teach the Word with clarity and conviction that made complicated truths accessible. God used him and those early lessons to shape the rest of my life in ways I could not have anticipated at the time.

We learned how to share the Gospel with love rather than pressure. We learned how to approach people with compassion rather than arrogance. We learned how to pray with expectation and study with diligence. We learned how to listen to the Holy Spirit and follow His lead even when it felt uncomfortable or unfamiliar. These were not abstract lessons taught in classrooms. These were practical skills forged in real encounters with real people who had real needs.

Slowly, the Word moved from my head into my spirit. It stopped being information I had collected and became truth I had internalized. The difference between those two things is enormous. Information can be forgotten. Truth that has moved into your spirit becomes part of who you are.

But learning is only the beginning. Obedience is the test. And God always tests what you claim to believe. He does not let you hold convictions in theory without giving you opportunities to live them out in practice. My test came sooner than I expected, and it came in a place I would never have chosen.

My test came on the steps of Hovey Hall.

THE DAY FEAR HAD TO BOW

It was a clear spring afternoon on ISU's campus. The sun was warm, and students were scattered across the quad, enjoying the weather between classes. I carried Bible tracts in one hand and flyers for our Sunday campus service in the other. Nothing dramatic. Just simple obedience to the assignment I had been given.

Then I saw them.

Five huge football players sitting on the steps of Hovey Hall. These were not average-sized men. They were giants by any measure. Six foot five. Six foot eight. Three hundred pounds and more of solid muscle built for collision and dominance. They sat like kings on a throne, surrounded by beautiful women who hung on their every word. They looked like they owned the campus and everything on it.

Everything in me wanted to keep walking. Every instinct screamed at me to find another route, another group, another opportunity that felt less intimidating. My mind immediately began constructing reasonable arguments for retreat:

They will not listen. They have everything they could want. They are not interested in religion or church services or anything I have to offer. Look at them. They are on top of the world. Why would they care about what some guy with Bible tracts has to say?

It sounded reasonable. It sounded wise. It sounded like common sense.

It was also fear wearing a disguise.

Fear began negotiating with my obedience. It offered compromises and alternatives. "You can witness to someone else. You can come back another time. You can find people who look more receptive." Fear is a skilled negotiator, and it knows exactly which arguments will sound most convincing to your particular mind.

But obedience began whispering too. It reminded me of the verses I had memorized. It reminded me of the commitment I had made. It reminded me that God had not called me to witness only when it felt comfortable.

My heart pounded so hard I could feel it in my throat. My legs felt heavy, as if invisible weights had been attached to my ankles. My mind continued its desperate search for justification to turn away. But God nudged me. It was a soft push. A quiet insistence that would not relent. *Keep going. Do not stop. Trust Me.*

I took another step. Then another. Halfway up those steps, I almost bailed. I almost turned around and walked away, convincing myself I would find a better opportunity later. But before I could make my escape, the biggest one spoke up.

"Hey, little fella. What you got there?"

I was six foot one and on the track team. I was not a small man by any standard measure. But standing before these giants, I felt like a child. And when I opened my mouth to respond, my voice betrayed me completely. It came out as a squeaky soprano that I barely recognized as my own.

"I'm, uh...passing out Bible tracts and inviting you to our campus service."

I waited for the laughter. I waited for the dismissal. I waited for them to wave me away like an annoying insect.

Instead, he smiled. "That's cool. Give us all some and talk to us."

And right there, on those intimidating steps, surrounded by men who could have crushed me without effort, God taught me a lifelong lesson that I have never forgotten.

God often sends you toward what intimidates you precisely because He has already prepared the hearts of the people you fear approaching. The obstacle that looks insurmountable from a distance often becomes an open door when you actually walk up to it. Obedience breaks fear. Once I stepped out in faith, God did the rest. He had gone before me and prepared their hearts to receive what I had to share.

From that day on, fear lost its grip on me. It did not disappear entirely. Fear still whispered its objections and offered its reasonable alternatives. But it no longer controlled my decisions. I had learned that obedience was stronger than fear, and that lesson changed everything about how I approached ministry.

LEARNING TO FIGHT FOR SOULS

That experience on the steps of Hovey Hall made me bold in ways I had never been before. I had tasted victory over fear, and I wanted more. I had seen God move in response to simple obedience, and I wanted to see Him move again and again.

Eventually, I took over leadership of F.A.T. from my brother Michael. The responsibility felt weighty but right. We trained others to share the Gospel with the same practical skills we had learned. We prayed together before every outreach. We studied the Scriptures together so that our message would be grounded in truth rather than emotion alone. We encouraged each other through the inevitable rejections and celebrated together when someone responded to the Gospel.

We went where most believers would never dream of going. We did not limit ourselves to safe environments where people already agreed with us. We sought out the places where people needed to hear the truth most desperately. We even visited taverns on Saturday nights, always with the owner's permission, and shared the Gospel with people who were drinking and searching for something they could not name. People were more open than you would imagine. The drunk man at the bar was often more honest about his spiritual hunger than the respectable churchgoer who had learned to hide his emptiness behind religious performance.

God can reach anyone, anywhere. That conviction grew stronger with every encounter. No one was too far gone. No environment was too hostile. No heart was too hard for the Gospel to penetrate when it was delivered with love and backed by prayer.

The clarion call grew louder with each passing month. This was not a hobby I had picked up in college. This was not a side project I would eventually outgrow. This was not a special assignment given to a select few who possessed unusual gifts or callings. This was the mission of every disciple. This was the heartbeat of what it meant to follow Jesus.

But I learned something else just as important during those years of intense ministry activity. It is not enough to know what God expects. You must also understand what keeps you from obeying. You must identify the internal enemies that sabotage your effectiveness and deal with them honestly.

WHY SELECTIVE OBEDIENCE IS DANGEROUS

The Bible is full of examples of people who selectively obeyed God and lost everything as a result. Their stories are not recorded as curiosities from ancient history. They are recorded as warnings for every generation that follows.

Adam and Eve lost Eden because they obeyed God in most things but disobeyed in the one thing that mattered most. Saul lost the kingdom because he obeyed God partially but made exceptions when obedience became inconvenient. Israel lost battles they should have won because they followed God's instructions up to a point but then improvised when His commands seemed too demanding.

I had lived that way for years before I came to Christ. I had also lived that way in the early months of my faith, holding back areas I wanted to control, making exceptions for habits I was not ready to surrender. But as the Word filled my spirit and the Holy Spirit convicted my conscience, God confronted me with uncomfortable clarity:

Selective obedience is disobedience. And disobedience is dangerous.

If you stay in that place too long, you drift back into spiritual sleep. The awakening that felt so powerful begins to fade. The urgency that once drove you forward becomes a distant memory. God had awakened me once from years of spiritual slumber. I did not want to fall asleep again. I did not want to return to the numbness and emptiness that had characterized my life before I knew Him.

WHY YOU CANNOT STAY HOME

In Numbers 32, the tribes of Gad and Reuben approached Moses with a request that seemed reasonable on the surface. They had seen the land on the eastern side of the Jordan River, and it looked good for their livestock. They did not want to cross the Jordan with the rest of Israel. They were comfortable where they were. They liked what they had found. They wanted to settle down and enjoy the blessings without participating in the battles that lay ahead.

Moses responded with a question that still echoes through the centuries and confronts every believer who is tempted to settle for comfort over calling.

"Shall your brothers go to war while you sit here?"

That question refuses to let us hide behind excuses. It exposes the selfishness that lurks beneath our reasonable-sounding justifications. It reminds us that we are part of a body, and when some members refuse to function, the whole body suffers.

This dynamic plays out in churches every single week. In most congregations, a small group of faithful believers carry the weight of the ministry while others remain passive observers. The same people teach the classes, serve the meals, visit the sick, and share the Gospel. The same people show up early and stay late. The same people give sacrificially and pray fervently. Meanwhile, the majority sit in comfortable pews and consume without contributing.

The work gets heavy when carried by too few shoulders. Burnout sets in among the faithful. Frustration grows among the committed. The mission slows to a crawl when it should be advancing with momentum.

We are living in urgent days. The signs of the times are not subtle. False teaching is spreading through churches like wildfire, deceiving many who lack discernment. Violence is rising in our streets and in our schools. Families are breaking apart at alarming rates. Deception is increasing on every front, from media to government to entertainment. Darkness is growing bold in ways that would have shocked previous generations.

This is not the time to sit back and let others carry the load. This is not the time to treat church as a spectator sport. This is not the time to prioritize comfort over calling. This is the time for all hands on deck. Every believer must recognize their role and step into it with urgency and purpose.

God does not ask us to do everything. That would be impossible and overwhelming. But He does ask each of us to do something. He has given every believer gifts and abilities and opportunities that are uniquely suited to their place in the body. The question is not whether you have something to contribute. The question is whether you will contribute what you have been given.

You cannot answer God's call from the sidelines. You cannot fulfill your purpose while sitting comfortably in the stands. At some point, you must step onto the field and engage in the battle. The clarion call demands a response.

MINUTE MEN: A PICTURE OF SPIRITUAL READINESS

In early colonial America, a special category of militia emerged known as the Minute Men. These were not ordinary soldiers who showed up when convenient. These were men selected for three specific qualities that set them apart from the general militia.

They were chosen for reliability. Their communities could count on them to show up when called. They were not flaky or inconsistent. They did not make excuses or find reasons to stay home. When the call went out, they responded.

They were chosen for enthusiasm. They did not serve reluctantly or resentfully. They embraced their role with passion and purpose. They understood that something larger than their individual comfort was at stake, and they were willing to sacrifice for it.

They were chosen for readiness. They trained regularly so that their skills would be sharp when needed. They kept their equipment maintained and accessible. They were prepared to move at a minute's notice, hence their name. They did not need days or weeks to prepare. They were ready now.

That is the kind of disciple God is raising in these urgent times. Prepared through consistent study and prayer. Alert to the spiritual realities that most people ignore. Disciplined in the habits that produce strength and effectiveness. Responsive to the promptings of the Holy Spirit without hesitation or delay. Spirit filled and mission minded.

The devil hunts the unprepared. He looks for believers who have neglected their training and let their spiritual weapons grow rusty through disuse. He targets those who have grown comfortable and complacent, those who no longer expect spiritual conflict and therefore do not prepare for it.

But a believer who is rooted in prayer and filled with the Word and trained in obedience is not an easy target. Such a believer has weapons that work and knows how to use them. Such a believer can recognize the enemy's tactics and respond with appropriate force.

Jesus demonstrated this kind of readiness when He faced Satan in the wilderness after forty days of fasting. His body was weak from hunger and exposure. He was physically depleted in every measurable way. But His spirit was strong. His mind was sharp. His weapon was the Word of God, and He wielded it with precision and authority.

Every temptation Satan offered was met with Scripture. Not vague religious sentiment. Not positive thinking. Not emotional appeals. Scripture. "It is written." Three times Jesus spoke those words, and three times the enemy's attack was defeated.

This is what spiritual readiness looks like. It is not perfection. It is preparation. It is not never being attacked. It is knowing how to respond when attacks come. And attacks always come. The question is whether you will be ready.

THE LOVE THAT FUELS THE MISSION

My understanding of God's love deepened dramatically during my years working at Pontiac Prison. I supervised recreation for both the general population and the condemned unit, where inmates awaited execution. These were men who had committed crimes so terrible that society had determined they should forfeit their lives. Working among them day after day changed my perspective on many things.

One day as I prepared a sermon in my office, God interrupted my thoughts with a question that stopped me cold.

"Would you give one of your sons to take the place of a death row inmate?"

The question was not hypothetical. God was pressing me to consider the depth of His love by measuring it against my own capacity for sacrifice. I have sons whom I love more than my own life. The thought of losing any of them is unbearable. The thought of voluntarily surrendering one of them is unimaginable.

My answer was immediate and completely honest.

"No."

I could not fathom giving one of my sons for anyone, let alone a condemned man who had done terrible things to deserve his sentence. The very idea violated every paternal instinct in my body. I would die for my sons without hesitation. But I could not send them to die for someone else, especially someone guilty of heinous crimes.

And God whispered to my spirit, with gentle but devastating clarity:

"That is exactly what I did."

That moment humbled me in ways I struggle to express. It pierced through my theological knowledge and touched something deeper. It reshaped John 3:16 from a verse I had memorized into a truth that overwhelmed me with its implications.

God did what I would never do. He gave His Son. Not for the righteous. Not for the deserving. Not for those who had earned His favor through good behavior. He gave His Son for the guilty. For the broken. For the condemned. For people exactly like those men in the death row unit. For people exactly like me before I knew Him.

When that truth becomes real in your experience, evangelism stops feeling like pressure or obligation. It becomes privilege. It becomes the natural overflow of a heart that has been transformed by grace. We were once the lost item in God's lost and found. We were separated from Him, condemned by our sin, without hope and without help. And He rejoiced when we were returned to Him. He celebrated our rescue with the joy of a father welcoming home a child who was lost.

Love becomes our fuel for mission. Gratitude becomes our motivation for obedience. We share the Gospel not because we have to, but because we want others to experience the same grace that transformed us.

INTRINSIC MOTIVATION: THE HEART GOD WANTS

Psychologists distinguish between two types of motivation that drive human behavior. Extrinsic motivation comes from external sources like pressure, guilt, or reward. You do something because someone is watching, because you will be punished if you do not, or because you will receive something you want if you comply. Intrinsic motivation comes from within. You do something because you genuinely want to, because it aligns with your values, because it brings you joy.

This distinction matters enormously in our walk with Christ. Extrinsic obedience is exhausting, because it requires constant external pressure to maintain. The moment the pressure releases, the behavior stops. Intrinsic obedience is sustainable, because it flows from love rather than compulsion. It does not require someone looking over your shoulder to keep you faithful.

God wants disciples whose obedience flows from love, not obligation. He is not interested in religious performance driven by guilt or fear of punishment. He desires genuine devotion that springs from transformed hearts. When you truly grasp what Jesus did for you, the Great Commission stops being a burden you must carry. It becomes the natural response of a grateful heart that cannot keep silent about such good news.

This does not mean obedience is always easy or that you will always feel like sharing the Gospel. There will be days when fear whispers and flesh resists. But the underlying motivation shifts from "I have to" to "I get to." That shift changes everything about how you experience the Christian life.

THE DAYS WE ARE LIVING IN

Whether Jesus returns today or years from now, the signs Scripture describes are visible everywhere we look. These are not obscure prophecies that require special interpretation to recognize. They are plainly evident to anyone who is paying attention.

Wars and rumors of wars fill our news feeds daily. Nations rise against nations in conflicts that seem to have no resolution. Spiritual deception is rampant, with false teachers attracting massive followings by telling people what they want to hear rather than what they need to know. Wickedness is increasing as behaviors once considered shameful are now celebrated and promoted. Violence is rising in our streets, our schools, and even our homes. Love is growing cold as selfishness becomes the cultural norm. Families are breaking apart at rates that would have been unthinkable just a few generations ago. Persecution of believers is increasing around the world and growing more acceptable even in nations that once championed religious freedom.

These signs are not meant to make us fearful. They are meant to make us focused. They are not given to paralyze us with anxiety about the future. They are given to mobilize us for action in the present. The clarion call is not a call of panic. It is a call of readiness. It is a summons to prepare ourselves and engage the mission with appropriate urgency.

God is assembling soldiers for a harvest that is still ripe, despite the darkness that surrounds it. Perhaps especially because of the darkness. People who are lost and confused and afraid are often more open to the Gospel than those who feel secure in their comfortable illusions. The fields are white for harvest. The question is whether there will be enough laborers willing to enter them.

THE REAL BATTLE: WHAT HOLDS YOU BACK

Every believer faces internal enemies that hinder obedience and undermine effectiveness. These enemies are not external forces we can blame for our failures. They are internal realities we must confront and overcome with God's help.

Fear whispers that we are not capable, that people will reject us, that the risk is too great. Insecurity tells us we are not qualified, that others are more gifted, that we should leave ministry to the professionals. Shame reminds us of past failures and suggests we have disqualified ourselves from usefulness. Old habits pull us back toward patterns of living that we know are destructive but find comfortable in their familiarity. Comfort seduces us with the promise of ease and convinces us that sacrifice is for someone else. Comparison steals our joy by measuring our progress against others rather than against our own calling. Doubt questions whether any of this is real, whether God truly speaks, whether our efforts make any difference. Complacency settles over us like a fog, dulling our sense of urgency and convincing us that there is always tomorrow. Feelings of inadequacy tell us we do not have enough knowledge, enough training, enough experience, enough spiritual maturity.

I faced every one of these enemies in my own journey. Especially fear. Fear was my constant companion for years, always ready with reasonable arguments for why I should stay silent and safe. But the day I stepped toward those football players on the steps of Hovey Hall, something shifted in the spiritual realm. Fear bowed. Obedience rose. God moved in ways I could never have orchestrated.

The battle is often won in the moment you take the first step. The enemy's power is greatest before you move. Once you step out in faith, his grip begins to break. Once you open your mouth and speak the words you have been afraid to say, you discover that God was with you all along, just waiting for you to trust Him enough to act.

So let me ask you some questions that deserve honest answers. What fear stops you from obeying what God has called you to do? What excuse do you reach for when the Holy Spirit prompts you to action? What lie do you still believe about yourself, about God, about the situation you face?

You cannot answer God's call until you confront these questions. You cannot move forward while dragging chains you refuse to acknowledge. The clarion call requires not only hearing but responding. And response requires dealing with whatever holds you back.

WHY WE STAY ASLEEP

Looking back across my own journey and the journeys of countless believers I have pastored over the years, I can identify many forces that keep people spiritually inactive. Understanding these forces is important, because you cannot overcome an enemy you do not recognize. You cannot break free from chains you do not acknowledge.

Fear keeps many believers from stepping into their calling. They fear failure, afraid they will try to serve and make mistakes that embarrass them. They fear rejection, worried that people will not respond positively to their efforts. They fear inadequacy, convinced they do not have enough training or enough knowledge or enough natural ability. Fear whispers a thousand reasons why they should stay safely in the pew rather than risk anything for the Kingdom.

Discomfort holds others back. The Christian life is not meant to be comfortable in the way our culture defines comfort. Following Jesus requires sacrifice and service and sometimes suffering. For those who have made comfort their primary value, the demands of discipleship feel threatening. They would rather remain passive and comfortable than engage and be stretched.

Apathy has settled over many believers like a fog. They simply do not care deeply about spiritual things anymore. The passion they may have once felt has cooled. The urgency that once marked their faith has faded. They go through the motions out of habit but feel nothing driving them toward action. Apathy is a dangerous condition, because the apathetic person is not even motivated to seek change.

Bad theology convinces some believers that their passivity is actually spiritual maturity. They have been taught, or have taught themselves, that grace means they do not need to do anything. They confuse rest in Christ with laziness in the Kingdom. They twist the truth of salvation by grace alone into an excuse for never responding to God's commands with obedience.

Confusion about calling leaves many believers uncertain about what they are supposed to do. They know they should be doing something, but they do not know what. No one has helped them discover their gifts or identify their place in the body. They are willing in theory but paralyzed by lack of direction.

Lack of discipleship is perhaps the most common reason believers remain passive. They came to faith but were never trained. They made a decision but were never developed. They started the journey but were never shown the path. Churches have often been good at evangelism but poor at formation. We get people saved and then leave them to figure out the rest on their own.

Complacency sets in when believers become satisfied with their current spiritual condition. They compare themselves to others who seem worse and conclude they are doing well enough. They mistake the absence of obvious sin for the presence of genuine growth. They settle for a Christianity that asks nothing of them and gives them just enough religious feeling to quiet their consciences.

Personal pursuits overshadow spiritual purpose when believers allow career ambitions, family activities, hobbies, entertainment, and endless busyness to crowd out their engagement with God's mission. These things are not necessarily bad in themselves, but when they occupy all the space in a life, there is no room left for Kingdom work. The urgent crowds out the important. The temporary eclipses the eternal.

These forces, and others like them, keep people in the pew instead of on mission. They keep believers spiritually asleep even while they maintain religious activity. They prevent the Church from being what Christ called it to be.

But the moment God wakes you up, everything begins to change.

Awakening stirs hunger. You begin to crave what you once ignored. The Word of God becomes food rather than information. Prayer becomes conversation rather than ritual. Worship becomes response rather than performance.

Awakening stirs conviction. You begin to see your own condition clearly. The excuses that once seemed reasonable now appear hollow. The compromises that once felt acceptable now feel grievous. The Holy Spirit illuminates what you had kept hidden in darkness.

Awakening stirs direction. You begin to sense that God has a purpose for your life beyond mere existence. The vague feeling that there must be more becomes a specific recognition that God is calling you to something.

Awakening stirs calling. You begin to hear the voice of God addressing you personally, inviting you into partnership with His work in the world. The general truths you have always known become personal words spoken directly to your heart.

Awakening demands action. You can no longer be content

with passive observation. Having been awakened, you must respond. The knowledge you now possess requires a verdict. The invitation you have received requires an answer.

AWAKENING LEADS TO READINESS

The moment God awakened me at ISU, I felt something shift deep within my soul. It was more than emotion, though emotion was certainly involved. It was more than intellectual understanding, though my mind was certainly being renewed. Something fundamental changed in my orientation toward God and His purposes.

I knew He was not waking me up just so I could enjoy a better church service. The worship at that campus church was wonderful, and I learned to love passionate praise in ways I never had before. But God had not awakened me merely to give me better worship experiences.

He was not awakening me just so I could feel closer to Him emotionally. The intimacy I began to develop with God during that season was precious beyond words. But emotional intimacy was not the ultimate goal of my awakening. It was a means toward something larger.

He was waking me up to prepare me.

He was waking me up because He wanted to train me.

He was waking me up because He had work for me to do, and I could not do that work while I was asleep.

Awakening is the first step on a much longer journey. It is absolutely essential, but it is only the beginning. You cannot take the next step until you take the first one, and awakening is that first step. But awakening that does not lead somewhere becomes awakening that fades back into sleep. The new awareness must be channeled into new action, or it will eventually dissipate.

Readiness is the next step after awakening. God awakens us

so that we can be made ready. Ready to hear His voice clearly. Ready to obey His commands fully. Ready to engage His mission boldly. Ready to serve His purposes faithfully.

In the chapters that follow, I will share how God began shaping me from someone who merely believed into someone who was ready to respond. Awakening revealed the truth about my condition. It showed me that I was asleep, that I was passive, that I was drifting, that I needed to change. But awakening was only the diagnosis. Training would be the treatment.

Training revealed the truth about my calling. It showed me not only where I was but where God wanted me to go. It showed me not only who I had been but who God was making me to become. It moved me from awareness to action, from conviction to commitment, from understanding to obedience.

God was preparing me for something I never saw coming. He was shaping me for a mission I could not have anticipated. He was equipping me for battles I did not know I would face. And at the heart of all that preparation was a clarion call that would change everything.

The Great Commission was not meant only for the apostles or for professional missionaries. It was meant for every believer who claims the name of Christ. It was meant for me. It was meant for you. And answering that call requires more than good intentions. It requires readiness.

Once He wakes you up, the real journey begins. The sleep is over. The training starts now. And everything that follows will flow from what happens next.

JESUS' MISSION MUST BECOME OUR MISSION

Jesus was clear about why He came to earth. He came to seek and save the lost. That was His mission, stated plainly and demonstrated consistently throughout His earthly ministry. He did not come primarily to establish religious institutions or create moral improvement programs or reform political systems. He came to rescue people who were perishing.

His mission must become ours. Not because we feel pressured by guilt. Not because we fear punishment for disobedience. But because we love the One who saved us and we share His heart for those who are still lost.

The Great Commission is not a project to be completed. It is a lifestyle to be lived. It is not an item on a checklist. It is the heartbeat of a disciple. When your heart beats in rhythm with the heart of Jesus, you cannot help but care about what He cares about. You cannot help but weep over what grieves Him. You cannot help but pursue what He pursues.

If awakening is God calling your name and rousing you from spiritual slumber, then the clarion call is God giving you your marching orders. It is the assignment that follows the awakening. It is the mission that gives purpose to your newfound life.

Now that you are awake, you must ask yourself what you are going to do with your awakened state. Will you roll over and go back to sleep? Will you return to the comfortable patterns that kept you numb for so long? Or will you rise to your feet, take up your position, and answer the call that God is issuing to His church in these urgent days?

The clarion call has sounded. The question is not whether you heard it. The question is whether you will respond.

3

I'M JUST ONE PERSON
THE LIE THAT KEEPS US SIDELINED

I have met many Christians over the years who feel invisible. They sit in church services surrounded by other believers, yet they feel utterly alone in their sense of insignificance. They listen to testimonies of what God has done through others and wonder why He has never done anything remarkable through them. They hear sermons about the great heroes of the faith and conclude that such heroism belongs to a different category of Christian altogether. They feel small. They feel ordinary. They feel disqualified before they ever begin.

I know this feeling well, because I lived with it for years. Even after God awakened me at ISU, even after I answered the clarion call and began training for ministry, a quiet voice in the back of my mind kept whispering the same defeating message: *I am just one person. What difference can I possibly make? The problems are too big. The opposition is too strong. The needs are too overwhelming. Who am I to think I could matter in the grand scheme of things?*

If you have ever felt that way, this chapter is written specifically for you. Because one of the greatest lies the devil whispers to believers is that their lives are too small to matter. He tells you that your voice is too weak to be heard. He reminds you that your past is too messy to be redeemed. He points to your limited abilities and convinces you that God could never use someone like you to accomplish anything significant.

This lie is devastatingly effective because it contains just enough truth to sound reasonable. You are, in fact, one person. Your voice is, in fact, limited in its natural reach. Your past does, in fact, contain failures and mistakes. Your abilities are, in fact, finite and imperfect. The devil takes these undeniable realities and builds a prison of discouragement around them. He wants you to conclude that because you are limited, you are therefore useless. Because you are ordinary, you are therefore unnecessary. Because you are flawed, you are therefore disqualified.

But God has never operated according to that logic. Throughout Scripture and throughout history, God has consistently chosen the unlikely, equipped the willing, and empowered the humble. He has repeatedly taken individuals who seemed utterly insignificant by human standards and used them to shake nations, topple empires, and advance His Kingdom in ways that still echo through the centuries. God delights in taking what the world considers foolish and using it to confound the wise. He delights in taking what the world considers weak and using it to shame the strong. And He delights in taking "just one person" who is willing to trust Him and doing immeasurably more than that person could ever ask or imagine.

Let me start with a story that changed how I see the power of a single surrendered life.

THE POWER OF ONE: THE DESMOND DOSS EXAMPLE

On October 12, 1945, President Harry Truman stood on the White House lawn preparing to present the Medal of Honor, the highest military decoration in the United States. The recipient that day was unlike any who had received this honor before him. He was a man who had never carried a weapon into battle. He was a man whose fellow soldiers had initially mocked him and called him a coward. He was a man who had been court-martialed for refusing to touch a rifle during basic training. His name was Desmond Doss, and he would become the first and only conscientious objector to receive the Medal of Honor during World War Two.

When Truman placed that medal around Doss's neck and shook his hand, the President said something remarkable. He told Doss, "I'm proud of you. I consider this a greater honor than being President."

Think about the weight of those words. The President of the United States, the most powerful man in the world at that moment, considered it a greater honor to present this award to Desmond Doss than to hold the office of the presidency itself. What could possibly earn such a statement?

Doss responded with characteristic humility. He said simply that he was trying to live out Matthew 7:12, which says, "All things whatsoever ye would that men should do to you, do ye even so to them" (KJV). That verse, commonly known as the Golden Rule, had become the governing principle of his life. He believed deeply in the commandment "Thou shalt not kill," and his conscience would not allow him to take another human life under any circumstances. But he also believed in freedom, and he knew that young men were fighting and dying to preserve it. He could not in good conscience stay home while others sacrificed everything.

So Doss found a third way. He enlisted not as a soldier who would fight but as a medic who would heal. He preferred to call himself a conscientious cooperator rather than a conscientious objector. He would not kill, but he would serve. He would not carry a weapon, but he would carry wounded men to safety. He would not take life, but he would do everything in his power to save it.

His fellow soldiers did not understand him at first. They saw his refusal to carry a rifle as cowardice disguised in religious language. They harassed him, mocked him, and tried to have him discharged as mentally unfit for service. But Doss endured the persecution without complaint and continued to serve faithfully in whatever capacity he was given.

Then came the Battle of Okinawa, one of the bloodiest engagements of the Pacific theater. Doss's unit was ordered to climb a sheer cliff face called Hacksaw Ridge and take the position at the top. The Japanese defenders were dug in and waiting. As American soldiers reached the top of the cliff, they were met with devastating fire. Men fell all around, wounded and dying, while the survivors were forced to retreat back down the cliff to escape the onslaught.

But Desmond Doss did not retreat.

Under relentless enemy fire, with bullets tearing through the air around him and explosions shaking the ground beneath his feet, Doss stayed on that ridge. He crawled from one wounded man to another, dragging them to the edge of the cliff and lowering them to safety using a rope and a makeshift litter. Each trip back into the killing zone could have been his last. Each wounded soldier he retrieved was one more than anyone had a right to expect.

And with every man he saved, Doss whispered the same prayer under his breath. "Please, Lord, help me get one more."

One more. Just one more.

He did not pray for a hundred. He did not pray for victory

in the battle. He prayed for the next wounded soldier, the next life he could save, the next act of service he could render. And God answered that prayer again and again throughout that terrible night.

By the time the sun rose, Desmond Doss had single-handedly rescued seventy-five wounded men from certain death on that ridge. Seventy-five lives saved by one man who never fired a shot. Seventy-five families who would see their sons and husbands and fathers come home because one skinny medic from Virginia refused to give up.

He was just one person. Just one ordinary man with an extraordinary faith. But look at what God did through his willingness to serve.

The story of Desmond Doss is not unique in history. The pages of time are filled with individuals who started as ordinary and ended up accomplishing the extraordinary. Rosa Parks was just one tired woman who decided she would not give up her seat on a bus, and her simple act of courage sparked a movement that transformed a nation. Nelson Mandela was just one prisoner who refused to let decades of imprisonment break his spirit, and his perseverance ultimately dismantled apartheid. Norman Borlaug was just one agricultural scientist who developed high-yield crop varieties, and his work is credited with saving over a billion people from starvation. Viktor Zhdanov was just one Soviet health official who proposed a global campaign to eradicate smallpox, and his vision led to the complete elimination of a disease that had killed hundreds of millions throughout human history. Martin Luther King Jr. was just one Baptist preacher with a dream, and his words continue to inspire movements for justice around the world. Mozart was just one composer. Shakespeare was just one playwright. Their individual contributions changed the course of human culture forever.

And above all of these stands Jesus Christ. In His humanity,

He was one person. One man born in an obscure village, raised by working-class parents, trained as a carpenter, active in public ministry for only three years, executed as a criminal before the age of thirty-five. By every worldly measure of success and significance, His life should have been forgotten within a generation. Instead, His life changed everything. His death purchased redemption for humanity. His resurrection defeated death itself. His name is now above every name, and at that name every knee will eventually bow.

Never underestimate what God can do through you, even if you feel like just one person. The lie that tells you to stay sidelined because you are insignificant is a lie straight from the pit of hell. God has always done His greatest work through individuals who were willing to trust Him with their ordinary lives.

THE DAVID PRINCIPLE: GOD USES THE UNLIKELY

When I read the story of David and Goliath in 1 Samuel, I see far more than a boy fighting a giant. I see God delivering a message to every person who has ever felt too small, too young, too inexperienced, or too unlikely to matter. I see God reminding all of us that He looks at the heart rather than the outward appearance, and that His criteria for choosing servants has nothing to do with the criteria the world uses.

The story begins with Samuel the prophet being sent by God to the household of Jesse in Bethlehem in chapter 16. God had rejected Saul as king over Israel, and now Samuel was to anoint the next king from among Jesse's sons. Jesse had eight sons, and when he heard that Samuel was coming, he naturally assumed that one of his older, more impressive boys would be chosen.

Jesse lined them up for Samuel's inspection. The firstborn, Eliab, stepped forward. He was tall and strong and looked every bit the part of a king. Samuel took one look at him and thought, "Surely the LORD's anointed is before him" (verse 6). But God spoke to Samuel and corrected his assumption. "Do not look on his appearance or on the height of his stature, because I have rejected him. For the LORD sees not as man sees: man looks on the outward appearance, but the LORD looks on the heart" (verse 7).

One by one, Jesse's sons passed before Samuel. Each one seemed qualified by human standards. Each one was rejected by God. Seven sons paraded before the prophet, and seven times Samuel heard the same answer. *Not this one.*

Samuel turned to Jesse with confusion. "Are all your sons here?" (verse 11).

Jesse almost seemed embarrassed by his answer. There was one more son, the youngest, but he was out in the fields tending the sheep. Nobody had even thought to call him. Nobody considered him a serious candidate. He was just David, the shepherd boy, the afterthought, the one who did not even make the initial lineup.

Samuel insisted that David be brought before him. And when the young man arrived, still dusty from the fields, still smelling of sheep, God spoke clearly to Samuel. "Arise, anoint him, for this is he" (verse 12).

This is the David Principle at work. God chooses the unexpected, the overlooked, the underestimated. Even David's own father never imagined he could be king. Even his own family dismissed him as insignificant. But God saw something in David's heart that qualified him for greatness when nothing about his external circumstances suggested such a destiny.

David was not the biggest of Jesse's sons. He was not the strongest. He was not trained as a soldier or educated as a leader. He was a shepherd boy who spent his days watching over sheep in the wilderness. But in those quiet hours alone with his flock, David had developed two things that would prove far more valuable than size or strength or worldly training. He had developed skill with his simple weapons, the sling and the staff, and he had developed a heart that was tuned to heaven. He wrote songs of worship. He meditated on the character of God. He trusted the Lord, who had protected him from lions and bears when predators threatened his sheep.

Years later, when the armies of Israel faced the Philistine champion Goliath in the Valley of Elah in 1 Samuel 17, those qualities would prove decisive.

Goliath was terrifying by any human measure. He stood over nine feet tall, a giant whose very appearance was designed to intimidate. His armor weighed more than most men could lift. His spear was like a weaver's beam, its iron head alone weighing fifteen pounds. He had spent his entire life training for combat, and he had never been defeated. For forty consecutive days, morning and evening, Goliath strode into the valley between the two armies and issued his challenge. "Choose a man for yourselves, and let him come down to me. If he is able to fight with me and kill me, then we will be your servants. But if I prevail against him and kill him, then you shall be our servants and serve us" (verses 8-9). His voice thundered across the valley, and not a single Israelite dared to answer.

The army of Israel was paralyzed with fear. These were trained soldiers, men who had fought battles before, men who carried real weapons and wore real armor. But when they saw Goliath and heard his taunting words, they trembled and fled. They saw a giant they could not defeat and concluded that the battle was already lost.

Saul was among those who trembled. Saul, the king of Israel. Saul, who stood head and shoulders above every other man in the nation. Saul, who had the best armor and the strongest claim to be Israel's champion. Saul had the position and the equipment and the physical stature that should have qualified him to face Goliath. But Saul did not have the heart.

That is when David arrived at the camp, sent by his father to bring food to his older brothers who were serving in the army. David heard Goliath's challenge, and unlike everyone else, he was not afraid. He was offended. He was indignant that this uncircumcised Philistine would dare to defy the armies of the living God.

His brothers tried to silence him. They accused him of arrogance and of leaving his sheep unattended just to watch the battle. But David would not be silenced. Eventually, word of his boldness reached King Saul, and David was brought before the king.

Saul looked at this young shepherd and immediately saw the problem. David was too young, too small, too inexperienced. Goliath had been a warrior from his youth. How could this boy possibly face such an opponent?

But David's answer revealed the source of his confidence. He told Saul about the times he had protected his sheep from predators. "Your servant has struck down both lions and bears, and this uncircumcised Philistine shall be like one of them, for he has defied the armies of the living God." David continued, "The LORD who delivered me from the paw of the lion and from the paw of the bear will deliver me from the hand of this Philistine" (verses 36 and 37).

Saul offered David his own armor for the battle. It was the king's armor, the best equipment available. But David tried it on and found he could not move. The armor did not fit. It was designed for Saul, not for David. And more importantly, David did not need Saul's armor because he already had weapons he knew how to use.

David went down to the stream and selected five smooth stones. He put them in his shepherd's bag and took his sling in his hand. Then he walked toward the giant while everyone else watched in disbelief.

Goliath was insulted when he saw who had come to fight

him. He cursed David by his gods and promised to feed his flesh to the birds and beasts. But David was not intimidated by the giant's threats, because David understood something that Goliath and everyone else had missed. The battle did not depend on size or strength or weapons. The battle belonged to the Lord.

David declared his faith before the watching armies of both nations. "You come to me with a sword and with a spear and with a javelin, but I come to you in the name of the Lord of hosts, the God of the armies of Israel, whom you have defied. This day the LORD will deliver you into my hand" (verses 45-46).

Then David ran toward the giant. Not away from. Toward. He reached into his bag, took out a stone, slung it with practiced accuracy, and struck Goliath in the forehead. The giant fell face down on the ground, and David used Goliath's own sword to cut off his head.

The Philistine army fled. Israel pursued and won a great victory that day. And it all happened because one shepherd boy knew the size of his God.

That is the David Principle. God does not need the biggest, the strongest, or the most impressive. God uses the unexpected, the overlooked, and the underestimated. God looks for hearts that trust Him, and He does impossible things through people who believe He is capable.

WHY SAUL DID NOT FIGHT

The contrast between Saul and David in this story has always fascinated me. Why did the man who looked like a warrior refuse to fight Goliath? Why did the tallest man in Israel hide in his tent while a giant mocked his God and terrorized his army? Why did the king offer his armor to a shepherd boy instead of wearing it himself?

The answer reveals a crucial truth about spiritual warfare.

Appearance does not equal courage. Strength does not equal faith. Position does not equal obedience. Saul had all the external qualifications that should have made him Israel's champion. He had the height, the armor, the title, and the responsibility. But he lacked the one thing that mattered most. He lacked a heart that trusted God more than it feared the enemy.

Saul saw Goliath with human eyes. He calculated the odds according to natural mathematics. He measured the giant's size and the giant's weapons and the giant's reputation, and he concluded that victory was impossible. Fear gripped his heart because he could see no path to success.

David saw the same giant with spiritual eyes. He looked at the same circumstances, heard the same threats, assessed the same odds, and reached a completely different conclusion. David saw the giant and saw a target. He saw an enemy of God who had made himself vulnerable by his arrogance. He saw an opportunity to demonstrate the power of the living God before the watching nations.

The questions the two men asked revealed their different perspectives. Saul asked, "How can a boy fight a man like this?" His question focused on human inadequacy. David asked, "Who is this uncircumcised Philistine who dares defy the armies of the living God?" His question focused on divine authority.

Saul saw defeat before the battle began. David saw a cause worth fighting for. "Is there not a cause?" David asked when his brothers tried to discourage him (1 Samuel 17:29 KJV). That question echoes through the centuries and demands an answer from every believer who is tempted to sit on the sidelines.

When you believe the problem is bigger than your God, fear takes over. It paralyzes you. It silences you. It keeps you hiding in your tent while the enemy struts and boasts and advances unchallenged.

When you believe your God is bigger than the problem, faith takes over. It propels you forward. It gives you courage to run toward what others run away from. It enables you to do what looks impossible because you know the battle belongs to the Lord.

FACING YOUR GOLIATHS

Every believer faces Goliaths in their life. These Goliaths are not nine-foot-tall warriors armed with spears and swords, but they feel just as intimidating. They stand between you and the life God has called you to live. They mock you and threaten you and convince you that you cannot possibly win.

For some, the Goliath is crippling debt that seems impossible to escape. The numbers are overwhelming. The interest keeps accumulating. The hole keeps getting deeper no matter how hard you work, and the giant whispers that you will never be free.

For others, the Goliath is fear, anxiety, shame, or depression. These internal enemies can be even more terrifying than external circumstances because they attack from within. They twist your thoughts and poison your emotions and convince you that you are fundamentally broken in ways that cannot be fixed.

For some, the Goliath is an addiction or a habit that refuses to break despite years of effort. You have tried everything. You have made promises and broken them. You have experienced moments of freedom followed by devastating relapses. The giant of addiction mocks your weakness and predicts your failure before you even try.

For others, the Goliath is a broken relationship that seems beyond repair. The damage is too deep. The words that were spoken cannot be taken back. The trust that was shattered cannot be rebuilt. The giant of relational brokenness tells you to give up and accept isolation as your permanent condition.

For some, the Goliath is cultural pressure that demands you compromise your faith to be accepted. The world tells you that your beliefs are outdated, intolerant, and foolish. The giant of cultural conformity threatens to exclude you from opportunities and relationships unless you bend your convictions to match the spirit of the age.

For others, the Goliath is spiritual dryness or discouragement that has stolen your passion for God. The fire that once burned in your heart has dwindled to embers. Prayer feels mechanical. Worship feels empty. The giant of spiritual apathy whispers that you will never recapture what you have lost.

A Goliath is anything that hardens your heart against God or makes you run instead of stand. It is any obstacle that seems insurmountable, any enemy that seems invincible, any challenge that makes you want to retreat to your tent and hide.

But David teaches us how to face these giants.

First, look at the giant through God's eyes rather than your own. Do not measure the obstacle by your strength but by God's strength. Do not calculate the odds according to natural mathematics but according to supernatural intervention. The giant may be big, but your God is bigger. The problem may be real, but your God is able.

Second, remember your past victories. David did not face Goliath with no track record of God's faithfulness. He had already seen God deliver him from the lion and the bear. Those earlier battles had prepared him for this larger one. You have lions and bears in your history, too. You have moments when God came through for you, when prayers were answered, when impossible situations resolved in ways you could not have orchestrated. Remember those victories. They are evidence that the God who was faithful before will be faithful again.

Third, run toward the battle rather than away from it. David did not approach Goliath cautiously. He ran toward the giant while everyone else cowered at a safe distance. There is something powerful about aggressive faith that refuses to be intimidated. The enemy expects you to flee. Confound his expectations by advancing.

Fourth, use the weapons God gave you rather than trying to fight in someone else's armor. Saul's armor did not fit David, and it would have hindered rather than helped him. God has equipped you with specific gifts, experiences, and abilities that are designed for the battles you face. Do not try to copy someone else's approach. Use what God has placed in your hands.

Fifth, declare that the battle belongs to the Lord. Before David ever released that stone from his sling, he announced his faith to everyone within earshot. He proclaimed that this victory would not come from sword or spear but from the name of the Lord Almighty. When you face your Goliath, speak truth over the situation. Declare what God is able to do. Remind the enemy, and yourself, whose battle this really is.

Goliath fell face down in the dirt that day. Not because David was stronger than the giant. Not because a sling is superior to a sword. Goliath fell because the living God was fighting through a shepherd boy who trusted Him completely. Your Goliath can fall the same way.

GIDEON: WHEN GOD CALLS THE FEARFUL

If David's story demonstrates courage, Gideon's story demonstrates fear. And I find Gideon's story deeply encouraging precisely because he was so afraid.

When we first meet Gideon in Judges 6, he is not standing tall and issuing bold challenges. He is hiding. The people of Israel had been oppressed by the Midianites for seven years. The oppression was brutal and relentless. Every time the

Israelites planted crops, the Midianites and their allies would sweep through the land like locusts and destroy everything. The people of Israel were starving, scattered, afraid, and utterly discouraged. They had been reduced to hiding in caves and dens just to survive.

Gideon was threshing wheat in a winepress when the angel of the Lord appeared to him. A winepress is a strange place to thresh wheat. Normally you would thresh wheat on a hilltop where the wind could blow away the chaff. But Gideon was threshing in a winepress because he was hiding. He was doing essential work in a concealed location because he was terrified of what the Midianites would do if they found him.

This is the man the angel greeted with words that must have sounded like mockery. "The LORD is with you, O mighty man of valor" (verse 12).

Mighty man of valor? Gideon must have looked around to see who the angel was addressing. Surely those words were meant for someone else. Gideon did not feel mighty. He felt weak and afraid and overwhelmed by circumstances he could not control.

His response revealed his state of mind. He questioned whether the Lord was really with Israel at all. If God was with them, why had all these terrible things happened? Where were the miracles their fathers had told them about? It seemed to Gideon that the Lord had abandoned His people and handed them over to their enemies.

Then God issued a commission that must have seemed absurd. "Go in this might of yours and save Israel from the hand of Midian; do not I send you?" (verse 14).

Gideon's objections tumbled out immediately. "Please, LORD, how can I save Israel? Behold, my clan is the weakest in Manasseh, and I am the least in my father's house" (verse 15).

I have felt exactly like Gideon many times in my life. I have looked at challenges before me and felt completely inadequate to meet them. I have heard God's call to do something and immediately begun listing all the reasons I was the wrong person for the job. I have hesitated to take leaps of faith because doubt set in before I could even begin. I have allowed the devil to replay the tape of guilt, condemnation, and shame until I was paralyzed by my own sense of unworthiness.

Sometimes we punish ourselves long after God has forgiven us. We hold onto failures that God has released. We define ourselves by past mistakes that God has covered with grace. We disqualify ourselves from service because we cannot believe that God would use someone with our history.

But God did not see Gideon as fearful or unqualified. God saw him as a mighty warrior. God looked past the fear and saw the potential. God looked past the circumstances and saw the calling.

And God patiently walked Gideon forward through his doubts. When Gideon asked for a sign, God gave him one. When Gideon asked for another sign to confirm the first, God gave him that, too. When Gideon was still uncertain, God allowed him to overhear a conversation in the enemy camp that confirmed what God had promised. At every point where Gideon's faith wavered, God met him with reassurance and confirmation.

But in Judges 7, God did something else that seemed counterintuitive. Gideon had managed to gather an army of thirty-two thousand men to face the Midianites. It was not a large army compared to the enemy, whose forces numbered over one hundred thirty thousand. But at least it was something. At least they had numbers on their side.

God told Gideon to send most of the army home. First God reduced the force to ten thousand by allowing anyone who was afraid to leave. Then God reduced it further to just three hundred by observing how the men drank water from a stream. By the time God was finished, Gideon's mighty army had shrunk to a tiny band that was outnumbered more than four hundred to one.

Why would God do such a thing? Because God wanted it to be unmistakably clear that the victory belonged to Him. If thirty-two thousand Israelites had defeated the Midianites, the people might have believed they had won through their own strength. But when three hundred men routed an army of one hundred thirty-two thousand, no one could claim credit except God.

Gideon and his three hundred men went out that night with the strangest weapons imaginable. They carried torches hidden inside clay jars, and they carried trumpets. No swords. No spears. No conventional weapons at all. At Gideon's signal, they broke the jars, held up the torches, blew the trumpets, and shouted, "A sword for the LORD and for Gideon!" (Judges 7:20).

The Midianite camp erupted in confusion. In the darkness and chaos, the enemy soldiers turned on each other. They fled in panic, pursued by the Israelites who joined the battle once the rout began. The oppression that had lasted seven years ended in a single night.

That is what happens when God steps into the life of just one person who is willing to trust Him despite their fear. Gideon did not stop being afraid. He simply obeyed anyway. And God honored that trembling obedience with a victory that demonstrated His power to an entire generation.

If we are going to fulfill our calling as Kingdom Soldiers, we must face our fears, kill our Goliaths, and become the mighty men and women of valor that God knows we can be.

WHO IS A KINGDOM SOLDIER?

When people hear the word "soldier," they typically imagine a certain type of person. They picture someone with muscles developed through rigorous physical training. They envision uniforms and weapons and elite special forces who can perform superhuman feats. They think of young men in peak physical condition who have been through boot camps and combat schools and survival training. That is what the world means when it uses the word "soldier."

But that is not how God chooses His soldiers.

A Kingdom Soldier fights an enemy that is spiritual, rather than political or military. They are called to stand for Christ in a world that increasingly opposes Him. They are called to spread the Gospel to people who desperately need to hear it. They are called to encourage other believers who are growing weary in the battle. They are called to engage in the conflicts of faith that rage in the heavenly realms and manifest in earthly circumstances.

A Kingdom Soldier is anyone, regardless of age or background or physical condition, who has been born again and is willing to follow the will of God. The qualifications have nothing to do with how much you can bench press or how fast you can run or how many degrees hang on your wall. The qualifications are spiritual, and they are available to everyone who belongs to Christ.

A Kingdom Soldier can be an elderly grandmother who has spent decades learning to pray with power and persistence. A Kingdom Soldier can be a young mother who is raising children to know and love Jesus in an increasingly hostile culture. A Kingdom Soldier can be a businessman who uses his platform and resources to advance the Gospel. A Kingdom Soldier can be a janitor who cleans buildings with excellence as an act of worship and shares Christ with anyone who will listen. A Kingdom Soldier can be a professor who challenges students to think deeply about faith and reason. A Kingdom Soldier can be an athlete who uses their influence to point others toward Christ. A Kingdom Soldier can be a teacher who shapes young minds during the most formative years of life. A Kingdom

Soldier can be a retiree who finally has time to devote to ministry without the constraints of a full-time job.

Your uniform as a Kingdom Soldier is not made of fabric and metal. It is the spiritual armor that Paul describes in Ephesians 6. Your belt is truth, the foundational commitment to what is real and right that holds everything else together. Your breastplate is righteousness, the character of Christ that protects your heart from condemnation and accusation. Your shoes are the readiness that comes from the Gospel of peace, the prepared stance of someone who is always ready to move when God directs. Your shield is faith, the active trust in God that extinguishes the flaming arrows the enemy hurls at you. Your helmet is salvation, the assured knowledge of your standing before God that protects your mind from doubt and despair. Your sword is the Word of God, the offensive weapon that speaks truth into every situation and defeats every lie. And underlying all of it is prayer, the constant communication with your Commander that keeps you aligned with His will and dependent on His strength.

Your mission as a Kingdom Soldier is entirely spiritual. You are chosen by God before the foundation of the world. You are forgiven through the blood of Jesus Christ. You are loved with an everlasting love that nothing can separate you from. You are empowered by the Holy Spirit who dwells within you. You are filled with resurrection power that raised Christ from the dead.

God is not looking for perfection. If He were, He would have no soldiers at all, because none of us are perfect. God is looking for availability. He is looking for people who will show up, who will say yes, who will step forward when others step back. God can work with weakness. He has demonstrated throughout Scripture that His power is made perfect in weakness. But God cannot work with unwillingness. He will not force anyone to serve. He invites, He calls, He equips, but He does not compel.

And whether you realize it or not, you are already in the fight. The devil does not give exemptions. He does not skip over certain believers because they have chosen to remain inactive. He attacks active believers and inactive believers with equal ferocity. The difference is that Kingdom Soldiers fight back with spiritual weapons, while passive believers suffer casualties without resistance.

IDENTITY: THE SECRET TO YOUR STRENGTH

The devil's first attack is always on identity. This pattern appears so consistently throughout Scripture that we should expect it in our own lives.

He did it with Eve in the Garden of Eden. His opening question was designed to make her doubt what God had said and who she was in relationship to God. *Did God really say you could not eat from any tree?* The question twisted God's words and undermined Eve's understanding of her place in creation. If the devil could make her doubt God's word, he could make her doubt God's goodness. And if she doubted God's goodness, she would be vulnerable to the suggestion that God was withholding something she deserved.

He did it with Jesus in the wilderness. Twice the devil began his temptation with the phrase, "If you are the Son of God." That little word "if" was designed to plant doubt about Jesus' identity. Jesus had just been baptized, and the Father had spoken from heaven declaring, "This is my beloved Son, in whom I am well pleased." The devil's strategy was to make Jesus prove what the Father had already proclaimed, to act out of insecurity rather than resting in the identity that had been given to Him.

And he does the same thing with you. The devil knows that if he can make you doubt who you are in Christ, he can make you live as though you are defeated, even though Christ has already made you victorious. He knows that identity determines behavior. If he can corrupt your understanding of your identity, he can control your choices and neutralize your effectiveness.

This is why it is essential for every believer to know and internalize what Scripture says about who they are. Not who they feel like they are. Not who their past suggests they are. Not who their critics say they are. But who God declares them to be.

According to Scripture, you are a child of God. John 1:12 says that "to all who did receive him, who believed in his name, he gave the right to become children of God." You are not an orphan trying to earn your way into the family. You are a beloved child with full rights of inheritance.

You are a new creation. 2 Corinthians 5:17 declares, "If anyone is in Christ, he is a new creation. The old has passed away; behold, the new has come." Your past does not define you. Your failures do not determine your future. You have been made new from the inside out.

You are forgiven. Ephesians 1:7 tells us that "in him we have redemption through his blood, the forgiveness of our trespasses, according to the riches of his grace." Every sin you have ever committed and every sin you will ever commit has been paid for by the blood of Jesus. You do not carry the weight of your guilt anymore. It has been removed as far as the east is from the west.

You are righteous in Christ. 2 Corinthians 5:21 reveals that God "made him to be sin who knew no sin, so that in him we might become the righteousness of God." You do not have to earn righteousness through perfect performance. The righteousness of Christ has been credited to your account through faith.

You are more than a conqueror. Romans 8:37 assures us that "in all things we are more than conquerors through him who loved us." Not barely surviving. Not scraping by with minimal victory. More than conquerors through the love of Christ.

You are seated with Christ in heavenly places. Ephesians 2:6 declares that God "raised us up with him and seated us with him in the heavenly places in Christ Jesus." Your position is not down in the dirt struggling to survive. Your position is enthroned with Christ, far above every principality and power.

You are filled with the Spirit. 1 Corinthians 6:19 reminds us that our bodies are temples of the Holy Spirit who is in us, whom we have received from God. The same Spirit who raised Christ from the dead lives inside of you right now. You are never alone. You are never without power. You are never without guidance.

You are chosen, royal, and set apart. 1 Peter 2:9 calls believers "a chosen race, a royal priesthood, a holy nation, a people for his own possession." You were handpicked by the King of the universe to belong to Him and represent Him in this world.

You are protected by God. Psalm 91 describes the divine protection available to those who dwell in the shelter of the Most High. "A thousand may fall at your side, ten thousand at your right hand, but it will not come near you" (verse 7). The angel armies of heaven are commissioned "to guard you in all your ways" (verse 11).

Spiritual warfare is not primarily about shouting louder than the enemy. It is not about more dramatic prayers or more intense emotional experiences. Spiritual warfare is fundamentally about standing firmer in who you are in Christ. When you know your identity and refuse to be moved from it, the enemy's attacks lose their power. He cannot make you feel defeated when you know you are victorious. He cannot make you feel worthless when you know you are treasured. He cannot make you feel hopeless when you know you are destined for glory.

YOU ARE NOT JUST ONE PERSON

David was just one person. A shepherd boy with a sling and five smooth stones. But he faced a giant and watched him fall because he knew that his God was greater than any enemy.

Gideon was just one person. A fearful man hiding in a winepress, convinced that he was the least qualified person in his family for any significant task. But he led three hundred men to victory over an army that outnumbered them beyond reason because God was fighting through him.

Desmond Doss was just one person. A skinny medic who refused to carry a weapon, mocked by his fellow soldiers, dismissed as a coward by men who did not understand his convictions. But he saved seventy-five lives on a bloody ridge because he kept praying for one more.

Jesus, in His humanity, was one person. A carpenter's son from Nazareth, born in a stable, raised in obscurity, rejected by the religious establishment of His day. But His life, death, and resurrection changed the course of human history and opened the way of salvation for all who believe.

So are you. You are just one person.

But God lives in you. The same God who empowered David and Gideon and Doss and countless others throughout history now dwells in you through His Spirit. The same power that raised Christ from the dead is at work in you. The same authority that commands angel armies is available to you through prayer.

And that changes everything.

You are not defined by your fear, though you may feel afraid. You are not defined by your past, though you may have failed. You are not defined by your weaknesses, though you may feel inadequate. You are not defined by your limitations, though you may see all the ways you fall short. You are defined by the God who chose you before time began. You are defined by the Christ who died to redeem you. You are defined by the Spirit who sealed you and empowers you for service.

So take out a piece of paper and write down every excuse you have used to avoid stepping into your calling. Write down every reason you have told yourself that God could not use someone like you. Write down every fear that has kept you on the sidelines while others engaged in the battle.

Then beside each excuse, write a Scripture that speaks to it. Replace the lie of fear with the truth of faith. Replace the lie of limitation with the truth of your identity in Christ. Replace the lie of disqualification with the truth of God's choosing and equipping.

When you believe the lie that you are just one person, too small to matter and too weak to make a difference, the enemy has won without a fight. But when you embrace the truth that the Creator of the universe has chosen to work through you, the enemy trembles. Because history has proven again and again that God plus one willing person is an unstoppable force.

You are a Kingdom Soldier. Not because you volunteered for impressive duty, but because you were drafted by the King Himself the moment you surrendered your life to Christ.

You are assigned. God has specific work for you to do that no one else can do in exactly the way you can do it. Your place in the body of Christ is not accidental. Your gifts and experiences and relationships have prepared you for assignments that are waiting for you.

You are empowered. The Holy Spirit who lives in you is the same Spirit who hovered over the waters at creation, who parted the Red Sea, who raised dry bones to life, who descended at Pentecost. That power is available to you.

And with God, you are more than enough. Not because of anything in yourself, but because of everything in Him. Your adequacy is not the point. His sufficiency is the point. And He is more than sufficient for whatever He has called you to face.

Stop believing the lie that keeps you sidelined. Stop accepting the devil's whispered suggestions that your life is too small to matter. Stop comparing yourself to others and concluding that they are qualified while you are not.

Rise up. Step forward. Answer the call.

You are just one person. And that is exactly what God is looking for.

In the next section, we will begin to look at the "basic training" of a Kingdom Soldier. It's one thing to enlist; it's another to be trained for battle.

PART II

BASIC TRAINING

4

MEETING YOUR COMMANDER

There is a moment in every soldier's life when he realizes that survival and victory depend on one thing: recognizing the voice of the commander.

A seasoned soldier once told me, "In battle, I don't move until I hear the commander's voice." He went on to explain how the noise of war overwhelms the senses. Gunfire erupts without warning. Orders are shouted. Adrenaline surges. In those moments, instinct alone can be deadly. So he trained himself to listen for one sound above all the rest. The commander's voice meant direction. It meant protection. It meant life.

"If I follow my instincts," he said, "I could walk straight into enemy fire. But when I follow orders, I stay alive and on mission." That image stayed with me, because it describes the spiritual life with unsettling accuracy. The battlefield of life is loud. Fear shouts. Desire pulls. Pressure demands immediate action. And if I move based on emotion or impulse, I can easily find myself wounded, exhausted, or fighting the wrong battle altogether.

Jesus is my Commander in Chief. My victory does not depend on intensity, sincerity, or good intentions. It depends on hearing His voice above all others. If I want to live as a Kingdom Soldier, I cannot be governed by emotion or driven by instinct alone. I must learn to move when He speaks and remain still when He is silent. I must learn obedience.

Jesus said, "My sheep hear my voice, and I know them, and they follow me" (John 10:27). Paul added, "Share in suffering as a good soldier of Christ Jesus" (2 Timothy 2:3). Those two statements shape my entire life. I am not wandering through existence hoping for spiritual success. I am under command. I belong to a King. I serve within His Kingdom. Everything begins there.

UNDERSTANDING THE KING AND HIS KINGDOM

Before I can follow Jesus into battle, I have to understand the Kingdom He represents. The more I study Scripture, the clearer it becomes that Jesus did not come to establish a religion. He came to announce a government.

Dr. Myles Munroe described the Kingdom of God as "the governing influence of a king over his territory."* That definition shifted my understanding. The Kingdom is not primarily about rituals, meetings, or moral improvement. It is about authority. It is about alignment with the will, purpose, and rule of the King. To belong to the Kingdom is to live under His government.

This means that being a believer is not about personal preference. It is about submission. To live as a Kingdom Soldier, I must adopt a Kingdom worldview. Jesus made this unmistakably clear in Matthew 6:31–34.

---

* Dr. Myles Munroe. *Kingdom Principles: Preparing for Kingdom Experience and Expansion*, Destiny Image Publishers, 2009.

Therefore do not be anxious, saying, "What shall we eat?" or "What shall we drink?" or "What shall we wear?" For the Gentiles seek after all these things, and your heavenly Father knows that you need them all. But seek first the kingdom of God and his righteousness, and all these things will be added to you.

Therefore do not be anxious about tomorrow, for tomorrow will be anxious for itself. Sufficient for the day is its own trouble.

When He told His followers not to worry about food or clothing, He was not offering comfort language. He was revealing Heaven's priority system. Seek first the Kingdom. Trust the King to handle provision.

The Kingdom is not only a future destination. It is a present reality. And it becomes real in my life the moment I choose to submit myself to the authority of the King. That submission often requires a reset. I have to ask God to realign my heart and retrain my thinking, because if I misunderstand the Kingdom, I will misunderstand my role within it.

JESUS: THE KING AND THE MODEL SOLDIER

Before I can follow Jesus as Commander, I must see Him clearly as King.

His leadership does not resemble that of earthly rulers. He does not dominate through fear or control. He leads through truth, righteousness, compassion, and sacrifice. He conquered not by taking life, but by laying His own down. His authority is eternal. His reign is universal. His leadership is perfect.

When I study how Jesus lived, I see the clearest picture of what it means to be a Kingdom Soldier. He knew His mission and never lost sight of it. He lived fully under authority, listening constantly to the Father's voice. He moved in obedience rather than impulse. He confronted darkness with truth and power. He trained others to carry the mission forward. And He completed His assignment.

Jesus did not act independently. He said plainly, "I only do what I see the Father doing" (John 5:19, paraphrased). That is the posture of a true soldier. A soldier listens. A soldier trusts. A soldier obeys.

YOUR IDENTITY AS A KINGDOM CITIZEN

This is where everything becomes personal.

I am not only saved. I am a Kingdom citizen. I am a son of God, a soldier in His army, and an ambassador of Heaven. Citizenship changes how I live. It means I exist under the authority and protection of the King. It means I represent His government wherever I go. It means my life has purpose, not passivity.

Authority does not come from personality, strength, or experience. It flows from relationship. When Jesus sits on the throne of my heart, His authority works through my life. When I forget who I belong to, fear takes over. But when I remember, confidence rises. Identity determines action.

When I walk as a son, I stop living like a survivor. When I walk as a soldier, I stop living like a spectator. When I walk as a citizen of Heaven, the enemy loses ground.

LEARNING TO HEAR HIS VOICE

If Jesus is my Commander, then hearing His voice is not optional. It is essential.

Hearing God is not complicated, but it is relational. Jesus said He is the vine and we are the branches (John 15:5). A branch does not bear fruit through effort. It bears fruit through connection. When I abide in Him through prayer, Scripture, worship, and obedience, clarity grows naturally.

Abiding produces strength. Strength produces confidence. Confidence produces obedience. Over time, I learn the sound of His voice. And like a trained soldier who can recognize his commander even in chaos, I begin to discern God's leading amid the noise of life. The battlefield belongs to believers who can hear their King.

A SEVEN-DAY KINGDOM RESET

These simple steps helped reorient my life under command.

For seven days, I read Matthew 6:31–34 each morning and asked God to help me seek the Kingdom first. Each day, I asked Jesus one direct question: "Commander, what is one thing You want me to do today?" I wrote down the first thing that came to mind without analyzing it, and then I obeyed.

Obedience creates clarity. Clarity builds confidence. Confidence forms a soldier. When this posture becomes habit, something shifts. Life begins to feel ordered instead of frantic. Direction replaces noise.

FINAL THOUGHT: FOLLOW YOUR COMMANDER

Chapters 1–3 revealed why God calls us. Chapter 4 reveals how we follow Him. This is the turning point of this book. This is where belief becomes allegiance. This is where identity becomes action. This is where the call becomes a command.

Your King is speaking. Your Commander is leading. Your mission is unfolding. The only question that remains is whether you will follow His voice.

5

LEAVING THE TRENCHES

There comes a moment in every believer's journey when God whispers, *Move*. It does not matter how long I have been walking with Him or how much I have learned along the way. Sooner or later, I reach a place where staying put is no longer obedience. For a long time, I assumed spiritual growth meant adding knowledge and refining habits. But there are seasons when God asks for something different. He asks me to leave what is familiar, step out of what feels manageable, and follow Him into territory I cannot predict or control.

Many believers spend years living in spiritual trenches. I know because I have done it myself. Trenches are not evil. In warfare, they serve an important purpose. They offer protection, shelter, and a place to recover when the battle is intense. But trenches were never designed to become permanent homes. What once protected me can eventually imprison me if I refuse to move when the command is given.

There is a difference between being in a trench because the Commander placed you there and remaining in a trench because fear has convinced you it is the only safe option left.

Defense has a role in Kingdom life, but it is never the goal. At some point, God calls His people forward. He calls us to advance rather than hide, to trust His voice even when the ground beneath us feels uncertain.

That is why Peter's story has always spoken so deeply to me.

STEPPING OUT OF THE BOAT

Matthew 14:22-33 says,

> Immediately he made the disciples get into the boat and go before him to the other side, while he dismissed the crowds. And after he had dismissed the crowds, he went up on the mountain by himself to pray. When evening came, he was there alone, but the boat by this time was a long way from the land, beaten by the waves, for the wind was against them. And in the fourth watch of the night he came to them, walking on the sea. But when the disciples saw him walking on the sea, they were terrified, and said, "It is a ghost!" and they cried out in fear. But immediately Jesus spoke to them, saying, "Take heart; it is I. Do not be afraid."
>
> And Peter answered him, "Lord, if it is you, command me to come to you on the water." He said, "Come." So Peter got out of the boat and walked on the water and came to Jesus. But when he saw the wind, he was afraid, and beginning to sink he cried out, "Lord, save me." Jesus immediately reached out his hand and took hold of him, saying to him, "O you of little faith, why did you doubt?" And when they got into the boat, the wind ceased. And those in the boat worshiped him, saying, "Truly you are the Son of God."

Peter was caught in a storm. The waves were violent, the wind was relentless, and exhaustion had set in. The disciples were doing everything they knew how to do, yet fear still gripped them. Then Jesus came toward them, walking on the water. At first, they were terrified, mistaking Him for a ghost. But the moment Jesus spoke, something shifted. Peter recognized the voice.

"Lord, if it is really You," Peter said, "tell me to come to You."

Jesus answered with a single word. "Come."

And Peter stepped out.

Every time I read that moment, something stirs in me. Peter did the impossible. He walked on water. People often rush to his failure, but I cannot forget that he actually walked. He trusted the voice of Jesus more than the stability of the boat, and for a moment, he experienced what obedience makes possible.

The boat represented everything Peter could explain. It represented logic, routine, familiarity, and control. Stepping out of it meant releasing what felt manageable in order to trust what could not be guaranteed. Faith always begins where control ends.

I think back to standing on the edge of a high dive as a teenager. I remember how easily I jumped then, without hesitation or overthinking. Years later, as an adult, logic and fear replaced instinct, and what once felt natural suddenly felt dangerous. That is what comfort does. It convinces us that caution is wisdom and that staying put is maturity.

Peter looked at the storm, then at Jesus, and reached a simple conclusion. *It is safer with Him than without Him.* So he stepped out. He left the security he could analyze for the security he could only trust.

I have faced moments like that myself. Moments when God called me to speak when silence felt safer, to step into responsibility when staying comfortable felt easier, to leave situations that no longer aligned with obedience. Every time fear won, I stayed in the boat. Every time I trusted Jesus, I grew.

I do not want to spend my life rowing in circles through storms when Jesus is calling me to walk with Him on the water.

CALLED TO DO THE EXTRAORDINARY

Believers often forget that God intends His people to live extraordinary lives. Routine Christianity dulls expectation until obedience feels risky and faith feels optional. Yet Jesus never intended His followers to live small, contained lives. He intended the power of the Kingdom to flow through them.

Peter witnessed miracles long before he ever walked on water. He saw blind eyes opened, lepers cleansed, storms calmed, and the dead raised. But that night on the sea, Jesus invited him into the miracle. That invitation became a turning point. Years later, the same Peter would command the lame to walk and see entire cities transformed.

None of that would have happened if he had stayed in the boat.

There comes a moment when God says, "You have stayed here long enough." Deuteronomy tells us that Israel remained at the mountain far beyond what obedience required. Familiarity replaced forward motion. Eventually, God commanded them to move.

I recognize that pattern in my own life. There have been seasons when God stirred a holy dissatisfaction in me. Not a call to abandon faith, but a call to deepen it. Not a new salvation, but a new level of obedience. Advancement always requires leaving something behind.

You cannot move forward while clinging to the comfort you have already mastered.

FORGING YOUR FAITH

I used to dread pop quizzes in school. They felt unfair and disruptive, but they served a purpose. They revealed what had actually taken root. Spiritually, God does something similar. Before promotion comes testing. Faith is not proven by intention, but by obedience under pressure.

Peter's test was the storm. Abraham's was Isaac. Moses' was the burning bush. My tests often arrive quietly, disguised as uncomfortable instructions. *Speak to that person. Let go of that security. Trust Me here.*

Faith does not grow by waiting for perfect clarity. It grows by acting on what God has already revealed. When I refuse to obey at my current level, I do not remain neutral. I stagnate. Progress becomes motion without advancement, activity without transformation.

At some point, every believer must ask, "Do I want more?" If the answer is yes, then stepping out of the boat is no longer optional. It becomes necessary.

WHEN GOD STIRS THE NEST

Scripture often compares spiritual growth to the flight of an eagle. An eagle's nest is carefully constructed with two layers. The top is soft and comfortable. Beneath it are sharp branches and thorns. The comfort is intentional, but it is temporary.

When the eaglets grow, the mother begins to stir the nest. She removes the soft layer, exposing discomfort. The eaglets squirm, protest, and inch toward the edge. Eventually, they leap. What looks cruel is actually preparation. They were born to fly.

I have lived through seasons like that. Places that once felt secure suddenly became restrictive. Routines that once brought peace no longer satisfied. At first, I resisted. Then I realized God was saying, *You were never meant to stay here.*

Comfort can be a gift. But when it becomes a destination, it becomes dangerous.

LEAVING THE TRENCH SEASON

In World War I, trenches were essential for survival. But the purpose of the trench was never permanence. When soldiers stayed in the trench after the command to advance, that trench became a prison.

Spiritually, many believers are still sheltering in places God never intended them to remain. They learned to survive but forgot how to advance. Safety replaced obedience. Familiarity replaced faith.

I have learned that when God gives the order to move, staying still becomes disobedience. A trench season can train you, strengthen you, and prepare you. But if you refuse to leave it, it will eventually limit what God wants to do through you.

The Kingdom does not advance from hiding. It advances when soldiers rise, hear the command, and move forward in obedience.

A PERSONAL QUESTION FOR EVERY SOLDIER

Have you been circling the same ground?

Are you still in a place that once served you but no longer stretches you?

Has God been stirring your nest?

Has Jesus been calling you onto the water?

We are not called to remain where faith costs nothing. We are called to trust the voice of the One who leads us.

The boat feels safe.

But Jesus is safer.

EXERCISE: STEP OUT OF THE BOAT THIS WEEK

This week, take one specific step of obedience. Not a vague intention. A real action.

Ask Jesus, "Lord, what is my boat right now? What are You calling me to do?"

Then obey.

Make the call.

Start the conversation.

Forgive the person.

Apply for the opportunity.

Pray for the stranger.

Begin the assignment.

Release what God has already told you to release.

Do not wait for the storm to calm.

Do not wait for perfect conditions.

Do not wait to feel ready.

Your Commander is calling.

Your faith is being forged.

The water is beneath your feet.

It is time to leave the trenches.

It is time to step out of the boat.

6

KNOWING WHO YOU ARE
IDENTITY FOR KINGDOM SOLDIERS

One of the greatest battles of my life has not been fought with circumstances, people, or situations. It has been fought in my mind. Long before any outward conflict, there was an inward war over a single question: "Who am I, really?" Because the moment I lose clarity about identity, everything else becomes harder. Courage becomes fragile. Obedience becomes complicated. Calling starts to feel like pressure instead of purpose.

The enemy understands identity better than most believers do. He knows that if he can confuse who I am, he can weaken how I live. If he can distort the way I see myself, he can limit the way I step into God's assignment. And if he can keep me questioning who I am, he can keep me living beneath what God already declared to be true.

I began to notice a pattern in my own life. Whenever God called me forward, the same whispers showed up. *You are not ready. You are not qualified. You are not the right person. Who do you think you are?* The timing was too consistent to ignore. The attack on identity was never random. It was strategic. Because if the enemy can win the battle of identity, he does not need to fight on other fronts. A confused soldier will defeat himself.

Looking back, I see something God was doing at the same time. Before He sent me into deeper waters, He kept returning me to the foundation. Before He gave me new responsibility, He kept reminding me who I was. God does not send confused soldiers into combat. He establishes identity before assignment. He anchors the heart before He advances the mission.

THE EAGLE WHO FORGOT HE COULD FLY

There is an old story about an eagle raised in a chicken yard. An eagle egg somehow ends up in a coop, and when it hatches, it grows up surrounded by chickens. It hears chickens, watches chickens, and learns what life is supposed to look like by imitation. So it scratches in the dirt, pecks at the ground, and stays low because everyone around it stays low. The eagle is not trying to be rebellious. It is simply living according to the only world it knows.

The tragedy is not that the eagle behaves like a chicken. The tragedy is that it never learns what it is. It has wings designed for wind. It has eyes designed for distance. It was made for height. But because it does not know its identity, it accepts a smaller life as normal.

That story has stayed with me because it describes what can happen spiritually. A believer can love God, serve God, even obey God in certain ways, and still live grounded. Still live cautious. Still live small. Not because their salvation is fake, but because their identity is unsettled. They carry Kingdom life within them, but they live as if the dirt is all there is.

Here is what matters most: The eagle never stopped being an eagle. Identity did not change. Only behavior did. It was always what its Creator designed it to be. It simply did not know it.

That is why identity has to come before behavior. Identity does not begin with what I do. Identity begins with what God says is true. When I start to believe what God says, my behavior changes, not through guilt, but through alignment. When you know you are an eagle, you stop living like a chicken. When you know you are a son or daughter of the King, you stop living like an orphan.

IDENTITY IS A SPIRITUAL REALITY, NOT A MOOD

Paul said it plainly: "Therefore, if anyone is in Christ, he is a new creation. The old has passed away; behold, the new has come" (2 Corinthians 5:17). That is not an inspirational phrase. That is a statement of fact. It is a spiritual reality that remains true whether I feel strong or weak, confident or insecure, hopeful or tired.

For years, I lived as if the Gospel gave me a second chance instead of a new nature. I treated the Christian life like self-improvement. I tried to earn what had already been granted. I worked for acceptance that had already been secured. I strained to prove worth that Christ had already purchased. And that kind of striving does not make a soldier strong. It makes a soldier exhausted.

The Holy Spirit did not come to pile religious weight onto an already heavy life. He came to make me new. He came to re-form me from the inside out so that obedience would flow from identity, not from fear. That is why identity is not just information. Identity is power. When identity is settled, the soul stops scrambling. The mind stops negotiating. The heart stops living on trial.

When you know who you are, you pray differently. You repent differently. You handle correction differently. You face resistance differently. Not because circumstances are easier, but because the foundation beneath you is steadier.

IDENTITY ANCHORS YOU IN GOD'S LOVE

Insecurity has been one of the most persistent battles of my life. It has whispered that I am always one mistake away from disqualification. It has tried to make my calling feel conditional. It has acted like a quiet supervisor, watching for flaws, keeping score, and threatening exposure.

But the truth God keeps returning me to is not complicated. God did not call me because I was qualified. He called me because I was His. He did not love me because I was impressive. He loved me because He chose to love me.

Romans 8 says nothing can separate us from the love of God in Christ Jesus. Not death. Not life. Not powers. Not present struggles. Not future fears. Not hell itself. That means I am not fighting to be loved. I am fighting from love. I am not trying to earn a place at the table. I am learning to live like I already belong there.

A soldier who doubts the Commander's care hesitates. He second-guesses. He holds back. But a soldier who knows he is loved fights differently. He can move forward without performing for approval, because his worth is not on the line. His identity is secure.

IDENTITY DETERMINES HOW YOU HANDLE TEMPTATION

Temptation almost always begins as an identity attack. Satan did this with Jesus in the wilderness: "If you are the Son of God..." The enemy was not only tempting Him to eat. He was tempting Him to prove. To act out of insecurity. To step out of sonship and into self-justification.

That tactic has not changed. The enemy still tries to make believers live as if the Father has not spoken. He whispers that I am on my own. That I have to manage my image. That I have to earn my place. That I need a counterfeit comfort because God will not come through.

When identity is weak, temptation feels strong. When I forget who I am, I reach for substitutes. I try to fill needs God has already met. I try to quiet fears God has already answered. I start fighting battles in my own strength that were never meant to be fought that way.

But when identity is settled, temptation loses leverage. Jesus answered with Scripture, but notice what He never did. He never debated His identity. He never tried to prove His status. He stood on what the Father had already declared and simply spoke truth. That is the model for a Kingdom Soldier. Settle identity before the battle comes. Know who you are before the lies start flying.

IDENTITY RELEASES KINGDOM AUTHORITY

After the resurrection, Jesus said, "All authority in heaven and on earth has been given to me. Go therefore..." (Matthew 28:18-19). He did not only announce His authority. He delegated mission under that authority. He sent His people out as representatives of the Kingdom.

That does not make me a superhero. It does not guarantee comfort or ease. It means I am a citizen backed by the King. Authority comes from position, not personality. I have authority because I am in Christ, not because I have performed perfectly. Power flows through relationship, not hype. The closer I walk with God, the more my life aligns with His will, and the more clearly His power is expressed through obedience.

When identity is clear, I stop fighting like someone who might lose and start standing like someone who knows where the victory already sits. Not because I never struggle, but because the foundation is not up for debate.

If the enemy asked me today, "Who are you?" I do not need to hesitate. I am a child of God. I am forgiven through the blood of Jesus. I am a new creation. I am sealed by the Holy Spirit. I am an heir with Christ. I am a citizen of Heaven. I am who God says I am.

Identity is not arrogance. Arrogance exalts self. Identity submits to truth. Identity is simply agreement with what God has spoken.

IDENTITY PREPARES YOU FOR WHAT COMES NEXT

In the previous chapter, we talked about leaving the trenches and stepping out of the boat. But stepping out is not meant to feel like panic. It is meant to feel like alignment. I am not stepping out as a desperate man hoping God shows up. I am stepping out as a son of the King, a soldier under command, a citizen of the Kingdom.

When storms rise, identity keeps me anchored. When accusations come, identity answers. When discouragement hits, identity steadies. I might bend under pressure, but I do not break. I may stumble, but I do not stay down. Not because I am tough, but because grace is real and sonship is secure.

Before Jesus sends soldiers into battle, He establishes who they are. He did it with the disciples. He did it with Paul. He does it with every believer willing to listen. He settles identity first, because identity is the foundation every battle stands on.

A SEVEN-DAY IDENTITY DRILL

For the next seven days, I want you to practice agreement with God. Each morning, read one of these passages and speak one sentence of truth out loud. Not as a performance. As training.

Read John 1:12 and say, "I am a child of God."

Read Ephesians 1:7 and say, "I am forgiven."

Read 2 Corinthians 5:17 and say, "I am a new creation."

Read Romans 8:38–39 and say, "Nothing can separate me from His love."

Read 1 Peter 2:9 and say, "I am chosen and set apart."

Read Ephesians 2:6 and say, "My position is with Christ."

Read Acts 1:8 and say, "I am empowered by the Holy Spirit."

You are not trying to talk yourself into a better mood. You are training your mind to live under truth.

Because when identity is settled, you stop fighting for a place you already have. And once you know who you are, the next question becomes unavoidable: Who is fighting against you?

That is where we are going next.

$$7$$

KNOWING YOUR ENEMY

FOR A WHILE, HE IS HERE TO STAY

I learned something early in my walk with God: You cannot fight a battle you refuse to acknowledge, and you cannot defeat an enemy you do not understand. As Kingdom Soldiers, we are not called to live afraid, but we are called to live awake. There is a difference between fear and alertness. Fear paralyzes and turns inward. Alertness sharpens the senses and steadies the heart. Fear makes you hide. Alertness prepares you to stand.

Whether we recognize it or not, the battlefield is real. The enemy is active. And the war did not begin with us. This conflict started long before any of us drew our first breath, yet it presses directly into ordinary human life. Every believer is born into contested ground. The question is not whether you will be involved. The question is whether you will be prepared when pressure comes.

THE KINGDOM BATTLEFIELD

Scripture teaches that more is happening around you than what your eyes can see. We live in a world that trusts what can be measured, tested, and explained. But the Bible speaks of a spiritual realm that intersects daily life in ways both subtle and forceful. You cannot touch it with your hands, but you feel its effects constantly.

You feel it when temptation arrives already tailored to your weakness.

You feel it when anxiety rises without a clear cause.

You feel it when a minor conflict suddenly turns dark, heavy, and destructive.

Paul names this reality plainly:

> We wrestle not against flesh and blood, but against principalities, against powers, against the rulers of the darkness of this world, against spiritual wickedness in high places.
>
> — EPHESIANS 6:12 KJV

That verse reframed everything for me. For a long time, I believed my battles were with people. When someone hurt me, I treated them like the enemy. When circumstances closed in, I treated the situation like the adversary. I fought personalities, history, disappointment, and pressure, all while missing the deeper conflict underneath.

Scripture gives us a powerful picture of this unseen battle in the story of Elisha and his servant. When the king of Aram sent horses and chariots to surround the city where Elisha was staying, the servant woke early, looked out, and saw the enemy army completely encircling them. He panicked. From his perspective, they were trapped. Outnumbered. Finished.

But Elisha remained calm. He said words that have echoed through history: "Do not be afraid, for those who are with us are more than those who are with them." Then Elisha prayed, "Lord, open his eyes that he may see." And God answered. The servant's eyes were opened, and he saw the hills full of horses and chariots of fire surrounding Elisha (2 Kings 6:15-17).

The enemy army was real. The danger was not imaginary. But it was not the whole picture. What the servant could not see was the greater force already in place. Heaven had not arrived late. It had been there all along.

That story taught me something essential. Fear grows when vision is limited to the natural. Confidence rises when God opens our eyes to spiritual reality. The battle looks overwhelming when you only see what is against you. It looks different when you see who is with you.

Over time, God opened my eyes in the same way. People are not the enemy, even when they wound us. Circumstances are not the enemy, even when they constrict us. There is a real adversary working behind the scenes, exploiting wounds, amplifying fear, twisting perception, and attempting to weaken believers from the inside out.

Until you recognize that, you will spend your strength on the wrong fronts. You will aim frustration at the wrong targets. You will confuse spiritual attack with personal failure. You will exhaust yourself fighting surface conflicts while the real war continues unnoticed.

When I surrendered my life to Christ, I did not only receive forgiveness. I stepped onto a battlefield. The enemy who once held ground in my life lost it, and he does not relinquish territory quietly. He cannot reclaim what Christ has purchased, but he will contest everything else. Your peace. Your clarity. Your authority. Your obedience.

Some believers want a faith that feels safe, contained, and predictable. They want Christianity to resemble a cruise ship rather than a battleship. But pretending you are not in a war never stops bullets. Ignoring the enemy does not reduce his activity. It only increases vulnerability.

The Kingdom battlefield is real. But so is the unseen army

that surrounds those who belong to God. And when your eyes are opened, you stop panicking at what you see and start trusting the One who commands what you cannot.

WHY YOU MUST KNOW YOUR ENEMY

General Douglas MacArthur is often attributed with saying that in war, you must know your enemy, his strengths, his weaknesses, and his tactics. That principle applies spiritually. You do not win wars by accident. You win by preparation, by clarity, and by refusing ignorance.

There was a season in my life when I was strong in worship but weak in warfare. I knew how to praise God, but I did not know how to resist the devil. I could lift my hands in church, but I did not know how to stand firm when my thoughts came under attack. I loved God deeply, but I underestimated the enemy's persistence. And ignorance cost me. Not because God failed, but because I was undertrained.

Paul wrote, "...lest Satan should get an advantage of us: for we are not ignorant of his devices" (2 Corinthians 2:11 KJV). That statement assumes something important. Mature believers are expected to learn how the enemy operates. Not so we become fascinated with darkness, but so we stop being surprised by the same predictable patterns.

The devil is not creative. He is consistent. He does not need new strategies, because the old ones continue to work. His methods have remained largely unchanged since the beginning.

He works through doubt, whispering questions about what God said and whether it applies to you.

He works through deception, twisting truth just enough to mislead.

He works through distraction, keeping you busy, hurried, and fragmented.

If he can make you doubt God's voice, believe a lie, or drift from obedience, he is satisfied. He does not always seek dramatic collapse. Often, slow erosion accomplishes the same goal.

TWO KINGDOMS, NO NEUTRAL GROUND

Scripture is unmistakably clear that two kingdoms are at work in the world: the Kingdom of Light and the kingdom of darkness. There is no third option and no neutral territory between them. Every life, every heart, and every decision is shaped by one authority or the other. Even when we try to avoid choosing, we are still being influenced. Neutrality is an illusion. Influence is unavoidable.

Paul describes what happens at salvation in direct, legal language. God "hath delivered us from the power of darkness, and hath translated us into the kingdom of his dear Son" (Colossians 1:13 KJV). That is not poetic imagery or spiritual metaphor. It is a transfer of citizenship. A change of jurisdiction. A believer does not slowly drift from one kingdom to another. The moment you belong to Christ, authority shifts. You are no longer under the rule of darkness. You now live under the reign of a different King.

That does not mean the enemy disappears. It means his access changes. He no longer owns you, but he will still oppose you. He cannot reclaim your soul, but he can contest your progress. He cannot cancel your salvation, but he can attempt to disrupt your obedience. His goal is not always to destroy faith outright. Often it is enough to dull it. To distract it. To keep believers busy, discouraged, or inwardly focused so the Kingdom advances slowly, if at all.

The enemy understands something many believers forget. He knows that you carry authority. He knows that the same power that raised Jesus from the dead lives within you through the Holy Spirit. He knows that when believers live awake, grounded in identity, and submitted to the Commander's voice, darkness loses ground. Influence shifts. Territory changes.

That is why the enemy works so persistently to keep believers confused about who they are. He promotes division because unity multiplies authority. He encourages passivity because obedience releases power. He feeds distraction because attention determines direction. A believer who knows who they are and lives under command is dangerous to the kingdom of darkness.

There is no neutral ground. You are either living under the influence of the Kingdom you belong to, or you are allowing the opposing kingdom to interfere with what God intends to do through you. The battle is not about ownership anymore. That has been settled by the cross. The battle is about influence, obedience, and impact.

And that is why knowing which Kingdom you belong to, and how that Kingdom operates, is essential for every Kingdom Soldier.

THE ENEMY'S CHARACTER AND STRATEGY

Scripture does not leave us guessing about who the enemy is or how he operates. The Bible describes his character with striking consistency, not to frighten us, but to keep us from being naïve.

The enemy is a deceiver. Lying is not a tactic he pulls out in extreme situations. It is his native language. Jesus said there is no truth in him, and whenever he speaks, he speaks out of his own nature. That means lies are not simply things he says. They are the atmosphere he tries to create. He lies about God's character, about your identity, about your past, and about your future. And the most dangerous lies are often the ones that sound almost true.

He is also a thief. Jesus warned that the thief comes to steal, kill, and destroy (John 10:10). Sometimes the theft is obvious, but often it is subtle. He steals peace a little at a time. He steals joy by replacing gratitude with comparison. He steals time through distraction and delay. He steals confidence by keeping believers focused on weakness instead of grace. Rarely does he rush in to take everything at once. He prefers slow, unnoticed loss.

The enemy is a tempter as well (Matthew 4:3). He studies patterns. He pays attention to moments of vulnerability. He knows when you are tired, lonely, angry, or discouraged. He does not usually tempt you when you are strongest. He waits until defenses are low and pressures are high. Temptation is rarely about the thing itself. It is about escape, relief, or control when trust feels difficult.

He is also an accuser (Revelation 12:10; Zechariah 3:1). Even after sin has been confessed and forgiven, he presses shame. He reminds you of what God has already released. He wants believers to live as though grace were temporary and forgiveness were fragile. His goal is to keep you bowed under condemnation so you never stand fully in your authority.

At the same time, Scripture is clear about his limits. He is not omnipresent. He is not all-knowing. He cannot read your mind the way God can. He is a created being, not an equal opposite of God. But he is observant and patient. He watches habits, wounds, fears, and fatigue. He learns what triggers doubt and what weakens resolve. His primary battleground is the mind, because thoughts shape choices, choices shape direction, and direction shapes destiny.

That is why Peter warned believers to be sober and vigilant (1 Peter 5:8). Not fearful, but awake. Not anxious, but clearheaded. Not obsessed with darkness, but attentive to reality. A sober mind recognizes lies when they appear. A vigilant heart notices when pressure is trying to push it off course.

Awareness is not paranoia. It is maturity. And maturity is one of the greatest defenses a Kingdom Soldier can possess.

WHY THE ENEMY HATES KINGDOM SOLDIERS

I used to wonder why some believers seem to face steady resistance while others move through life with relatively little opposition. For a long time, I assumed it meant I was doing something wrong. That the pressure, the setbacks, or the spiritual pushback were signs of failure or weakness. Over time, God helped me see the pattern more clearly.

The enemy does not waste effort on those who pose no threat.

Darkness resists what challenges it. The enemy is strategic with his attention. He targets lives that matter, obedience that counts, and believers who are positioned to advance the Kingdom. Resistance is not proof that you are losing. Often, it is proof that you are moving in the right direction.

Kingdom Soldiers are dangerous because we carry Heaven's authority. We do not fight in our own name or strength. We move under the authority of Christ, backed by His victory. That authority threatens the kingdom of darkness because it cannot be overpowered or negotiated away.

We are dangerous because we bear God's image. Every believer reflects something of the Creator. When we live in obedience, holiness, and humility, our lives remind the enemy of everything he lost and can never regain.

We are dangerous because obedience advances territory. Every surrendered decision, every step taken in faith, every quiet act of obedience pushes darkness back. The Kingdom does not only advance through dramatic moments. It advances through daily faithfulness.

We are dangerous because prayer disrupts plans. Prayer exposes schemes, blocks assignments, and calls Heaven's intervention into earthly situations. The enemy fears praying believers, because prayer shifts battles out of his control.

We are dangerous because testimony proves redemption is real. Every restored life, every forgiven sin, every healed relationship stands as evidence that grace works and darkness does not have the final word. Your testimony is not just a personal story. It is a declaration that the enemy's power is limited.

Every healed life, every forgiven sin, every restored marriage, every obedient step is an act of war against darkness. Your life is not merely about you. It is strategic in the larger conflict between two kingdoms.

So if you are experiencing resistance, do not assume you are failing. Ask a different question. It may not be a sign that something is wrong. It may be evidence that your life matters, your obedience counts, and your presence threatens the enemy's hold.

Resistance does not always mean retreat is needed. Sometimes it means you are exactly where you are supposed to be.

STANDING YOUR GROUND

This chapter is not meant to frighten you. Fear is a weapon of the enemy, and I will not hand it to him. This chapter is meant to prepare you.

When you know your enemy, you stop fighting the wrong battles. You stop blaming people for spiritual pressure. You stop being surprised by predictable tactics. And you learn to trust your Commander more deeply.

The enemy is real, but Christ is greater.

The war is intense, but the outcome is settled.

"Greater is He that is in you, than he that is in the world" (1 John 4:4 KJV).

The enemy is here to stay until Jesus returns and brings this war to an end. But so are you. You have been called, equipped, and commissioned. You do not stand alone. You stand with the saints, with the Church, and under the authority of Christ Himself.

The enemy is real.

But so is your Commander.

And His victory is your inheritance.

PART III

ADVANCED TRAINING

$$8$$

YOUR KINGDOM WEAPONS

TOOLS AND SKILLS FOR THE BATTLE

When a firefighter rolls up to a house fire, he never walks in with just a helmet and a good attitude. He does not park the truck, take a deep breath, and stroll toward the flames hoping for the best. He suits up.

Every piece of his gear matters, because fire is not sentimental. The coat. The pants. The boots. The gloves. The mask. The oxygen tank. The helmet. Missing even one piece can turn a rescue into a tragedy. And a firefighter does not learn his equipment in the middle of the flames. He trains long before the call comes. He learns the feel of the straps, the weight of the tank, the way the mask seals. He practices until he can suit up in the dark, in smoke, under pressure.

That is how I have learned to think about spiritual warfare.

You and I are not called to walk onto a battlefield with only a few Bible verses and a worship playlist. We are not meant to face the enemy of our souls with good intentions and vague hopes. God has already provided what we need. The question is not whether the gear exists. The question is whether we will put it on, learn it, and use it.

Scripture shows us that God is not surprised by conflict,

and He is not careless with His people. Judges tells us that the Lord intentionally left certain nations in the land, not to torment Israel, but to train them. These enemies remained so that a generation who had never fought would learn how. God did not remove every threat because He knew something Israel did not yet know. They were going to need discernment, strength, and dependence on Him. Victory would not come from comfort. It would come from learning to fight under His command.

That truth reframed how I understood resistance in my own life. Some battles are not signs of failure. They are signs of preparation. God is mindful of those who have never been engaged in warfare, and sometimes the presence of opposition is His way of teaching loyalty, obedience, and trust. He does not abandon His people in the fight. He trains them through it.

Too many believers live defeated lives, not because God has left them, but because they never learned how to stand. They treat spiritual warfare like an abstract idea instead of a daily reality. And when pressure comes, they are caught off guard. Confused. Overwhelmed. Not because God failed them, but because they never trained with what He already provided.

THE POWER BEHIND EVERY WEAPON: THE GOSPEL

Before we talk about armor, we have to talk about power. Before we talk about equipment, we have to talk about the source of everything we carry.

Paul wrote, "For I am not ashamed of the gospel of Christ: for it is the power of God unto salvation to every one that believeth" (Romans 1:16 KJV). Paul does not say the Gospel has power, as though power were something attached to it. He says the Gospel *is* power.

The Gospel is the announcement that Jesus has already

done what no man could do. Sin has been broken. Death has been defeated. A new Kingdom has been established. And when you came to Christ, you were transferred into it.

That changes everything about spiritual warfare.

You do not fight for victory. You fight from victory. You are not trying to persuade God to help you. You are not begging for rescue as though the outcome were uncertain. You are standing on what Jesus has already accomplished and learning how to enforce that reality in your life.

The Gospel is not a memory from an altar call. It is the living power of God working in you every single day. When you understand that, the armor makes sense. The weapons make sense. The training makes sense.

THE WHOLE ARMOR OF GOD

Paul makes the expectation clear. "Therefore take unto you the whole armour of God, that ye may be able to withstand in the evil day, and having done all, to stand" (Ephesians 6:13 KJV).

Paul is describing a soldier who expects contact. Not paranoia. Not fear. Reality. He is not halfway dressed. He is not casual. He is not choosing what feels comfortable today. He is equipped because his life depends on it.

God uses this image because too many believers are stepping into spiritual firefights wearing spiritual flip-flops. We are surprised by resistance. We act like the battle is unusual. We do not recognize attacks until we are already wounded.

The armor is not pressure from God. It is provision. It is mercy.

Let's walk through it.

THE BELT OF TRUTH: What Holds Everything Together

Paul begins, "Stand therefore, having your loins girt about with truth" (Ephesians 6:14 KJV).

For a Roman soldier, the belt was not decoration. It held everything in place. It supported the weight of the armor. It secured the tunic. It carried the sword. Without it, the rest of the equipment became unstable.

But the word *stand* deserves attention.

For a Roman infantryman, standing meant holding assigned ground. No retreat. No broken rank. Victory was often decided by who refused to move. A Roman soldier stood because of training, discipline, and resolve.

For the believer, standing means something different.

We stand in a finished victory. Christ already won. We are not standing to achieve triumph. We are standing to maintain what Jesus has accomplished. We stand in position, not performance. We stand against spiritual forces, not flesh and blood.

A Kingdom Soldier does not chase the enemy. He holds ground clothed in truth, righteousness, faith, and the Word.

Truth functions spiritually the way the belt functioned physically. It holds everything together.

This is not only about honesty in conversation, though that matters. This is about living anchored in what God says is true. Who He is. Who you are in Christ. What reality actually is.

The enemy's language is deception. When truth becomes foggy, everything else weakens. A confused believer is a vulnerable believer.

I learned this the hard way. When I forgot who I was in Christ, I became an easy target. After my first wife's death, when I nearly took my own life, the enemy was not inventing new lies. He was exploiting a wounded soul that had lost its grip on truth. God's love had not changed. But my ability to remember it had.

Truth must have the final word.

THE BREASTPLATE OF RIGHTEOUSNESS: Guarding Your Heart

Paul continues, "And having on the breastplate of righteousness" (Ephesians 6:14 KJV).

The breastplate protects the vital organs. A direct hit without it can end the battle immediately. Spiritually, righteousness guards the heart the same way.

There are two sides to this protection.

First, there is the righteousness you receive in Christ. When you trusted Jesus, God declared you righteous. Accusation does not get the final word. Shame does not get the final word. Your past does not get the final word.

Second, righteousness is how you live. Obedience matters because compromise exposes you. Unrepentant sin is not merely a mistake. It is an open door.

Scripture describes the heart as the core of a person's being. Mind. Will. Emotions. Beliefs. To guard it means watching carefully, like a sentry at a city gate. Not everything gets access, even if it looks harmless.

I can testify that guarding the heart is active, not passive. I have let my guard down too many times, and it came at a cost. When I stepped away from pastoring after eleven years, a decision made from emotion rather than truth, I learned again why the armor must be put on daily, not occasionally.

The breastplate is both rest and responsibility. Resting in what Jesus has done, and cooperating with what He is doing in you.

THE SHOES OF THE GOSPEL OF PEACE: Stable and Ready

Paul writes, "And your feet shod with the preparation of the gospel of peace" (Ephesians 6:15 KJV).

Roman sandals were built for traction. They kept soldiers steady on unstable ground and ready to move when commanded.

The Gospel of peace gives you both.

It gives you stability because you are at peace with God. You are not fighting to be accepted. You are not earning your place. When anxiety tries to tip you over, you have something solid beneath your feet.

It also makes you ready. Peace is not passivity. Peace is a Kingdom presence that moves into chaos and stands firm there.

THE SHIELD OF FAITH: Extinguishing Fiery Darts

Paul continues, "Above all, taking the shield of faith, wherewith ye shall be able to quench all the fiery darts of the wicked" (Ephesians 6:16 KJV).

The enemy still shoots flaming arrows. Condemnation. Fear. Doubt. Anxiety. Offense. These are not harmless thoughts. They are designed to burn and spread.

Faith is the shield that stops them.

Faith is not pretending life is easy. Faith is choosing to trust God's character and promises over the moment you are standing in. Sometimes that decision is quiet. Sometimes it must be spoken out loud. Either way, faith extinguishes what was sent to ignite you.

THE HELMET OF SALVATION: Guarding Your Mind

Paul says, "And take the helmet of salvation" (Ephesians 6:17 KJV).

The mind is a favorite battlefield. Thoughts shape choices. Choices shape direction.

The helmet of salvation is assurance. The settled reality that you belong to God. When the enemy questions your standing, salvation answers.

Putting on the helmet means refusing to rehearse shame that Christ already forgave. It means guarding your thoughts with the truth of the Gospel.

THE SWORD OF THE SPIRIT: The Word as a Weapon

Paul writes, "And the sword of the Spirit, which is the word of God" (Ephesians 6:17 KJV).

The sword is different. It is how you fight back.

Jesus modeled this in the wilderness. He did not debate the devil. He answered with Scripture: "It is written."

The Word is not just inspiration. It is issued weaponry. You learn it ahead of time. You store it. You speak it when pressure hits.

PRAYER: Communication with Headquarters

Paul immediately adds, "Praying always with all prayer and supplication in the Spirit" (Ephesians 6:18 KJV).

Prayer is not a bonus. Prayer is connection.

Armor protects you. Communication directs you.

Many of my worst decisions were made not because I lacked faith, but because I acted without checking in. Prayer slows reaction and creates space to respond. It keeps you aligned with the Commander instead of driven by emotion.

Prayer is our supernatural link to headquarters. I have lost battles by assuming I knew what God wanted instead of asking. The Holy Spirit teaches, guides, empowers, and instructs. We must trust Him to do His job.

A praying soldier is not passive. He is informed.

YOUR KINGDOM SKILLSET: Your Gift Is a Weapon

Every soldier carries the same basic gear, but not every soldier has the same assignment. The Kingdom works the same way.

Your gifts are intentional. Your instincts are strategic. What comes naturally to you may be how God intends to push darkness back.

A gift becomes a weapon when it is surrendered to Jesus and trained through use. Untested gifts stay dull. Practiced gifts grow sharp.

You do not need every gift.

You need to use the one you have.

That is how soldiers mature.

That is how battles turn.

That is how the Kingdom advances.

A 21-DAY ARMOR ACTIVATION CHALLENGE

I do not want this chapter to sit in your head like information. I want it to settle into your body like instinct. I want these truths to move from something you remember into something you do, something you reach for without thinking when pressure hits.

In a real emergency, no one has time to review notes. No one pauses to reread a manual. You move with what you have practiced. You rely on what has been trained into you. Muscle memory saves lives.

That is what I want for you here.

I want you to know how to suit up in the dark. When fear rises in the middle of the night. When temptation hits without warning. When discouragement presses in before you have time to pray a polished prayer. I want truth to be your reflex. Faith to rise automatically. Your mind guarded without debate. Scripture to answer lies before they settle in.

This kind of readiness does not come from reading once. It comes from repetition. From daily use. From choosing to put on the armor even on ordinary days when nothing dramatic seems to be happening. Especially then.

Battles rarely announce themselves ahead of time. They arrive suddenly, often when you are tired, distracted, or emotionally worn down. In those moments, you will not rise to the level of your intentions. You will fall to the level of your training.

That is why this chapter matters.

Not so you can talk about spiritual warfare.

But so you can stand in it.

Not so you can admire the armor.

But so you can wear it.

I want these weapons to feel familiar in your hands. I want obedience to feel practiced, not forced. I want response to replace reaction.

Because when the heat rises and the smoke thickens, the soldiers who walk out are not the ones who meant to prepare. They are the ones who did.

So let me slow this down and make it practical.

Readiness is not built all at once. It is formed in layers. First, you must be anchored in what is true about God and what is true about you. Then you must learn how to wear what He has already given you. Finally, you must step into active use, letting these tools shape how you actually live and respond.

That is how muscle memory is formed.

Not by knowing everything.

But by practicing the right things in the right order.

What follows is not theory. It is training.

We will begin by grounding you in the power that makes every weapon effective. Then we will walk through how to put on the armor piece by piece. Finally, we will move from preparation into action, learning how to use what God has given you in real battles, not hypothetical ones.

This is how soldiers are formed.

This is how confidence grows.

This is how readiness becomes instinct.

Why This Matters: Knowing the Purpose of Your Weapons

The late Dr. Myles Munroe once said, "Where purpose is not known, abuse is inevitable."[*]

That statement carries deep weight in spiritual warfare.

When I look back on how I once used the weapons God gave me, I can see seasons of misuse and misunderstanding. Roman weapons were designed to kill and to protect through physical force. Every piece of their armor existed for physical domination and survival.

But the believer's weapons are different.

They are spiritual, not physical.

Relational, not violent.

Transformational, not destructive.

When we forget that our battle is spiritual and not physical,

---

[*] Myles Munroe. *Understanding the Purpose and Power of Men: A Book for Men and the Women Who Love Them.* Whitaker House, 2001, pg. 43.

we begin misusing our weapons. We fight people instead of principalities. We use Scripture to wound instead of to heal. We rely on skill instead of faith. This is one of the enemy's oldest strategies: to erode our confidence in weapons that are not carnal but mighty through God.

Every weapon God has given you has already been battle-tested by Jesus Himself. They work. But they work when used for their intended purpose.

David understood this when he faced Goliath. His confidence was not in the sling. It was not in his accuracy. It was not in his experience. His confidence was in the God who would stand behind the stone released in faith.

David knew something many believers forget: The power was never in the weapon. The power was in the Lord who stood behind it.

Every time you use your spiritual weapons as they were designed to be used, you discover the same truth: The battle is not yours. It belongs to the Lord.

A Roman soldier put on armor to take life.

A Kingdom Soldier puts on armor to live the life of Christ.

Roman armor was metal on the body.

God's armor is Christ's character and promises wrapped around your heart, mind, and will.

Rome built an empire that eventually fell.

God is forming a people who belong to an unshakable Kingdom.

That is why this training matters.

Week 1: Gospel and Identity (Days 1–7)

Each day, read Romans 1:16 and one of the following: Romans 6 or 2 Corinthians 5:17. Thank God out loud for what the Gospel has done in you. Keep it simple and honest.

Say it plainly:

"I fight from victory, not for victory. I belong to You."

Let this week settle your identity. This is where confidence is born.

Week 2: Suit Up Daily (Days 8–14)

Each morning, pray through Ephesians 6:13–18 slowly and personally. Use your own words. Ask God to make truth steady in you, righteousness real in you, peace firm in you, faith active in you, salvation settled in you, and Scripture sharp in you.

This week is about familiarity, wearing the armor until it no longer feels foreign.

Week 3: Engage (Days 15–21)

Each day, choose one verse that addresses the pressure you are facing. Speak it when the attack comes. Not once. Repeatedly.

Then take one real step of obedience. A conversation. A confession. A forgiveness. A decision you have been avoiding.

End each day by writing two sentences:

Where did I feel resistance today?

Where did I see God help me?

This is where preparation turns into practice.

THIS IS how believers become trained soldiers. Not by collecting concepts, but by practicing obedience.

You are not a civilian. You are a Kingdom Soldier. God has armed you. He has given you everything you need.

Now it is time to train, to stand, and to fight well.

9

THE PARABLE OF
HIDDEN POTENTIAL

WHEN GOD CALLS YOUR NAME IN THE DARK

I have learned that every soldier faces a moment that shakes him. Not because the enemy suddenly becomes stronger, but because doubt finds its way in quietly. It does not arrive as panic or chaos. It arrives as a thought. A question. A hesitation that lodges itself deep inside and refuses to leave.

It is the moment when something whispers from the depths of your soul, something I once feared more than death itself.

What if God made a mistake choosing me.

What if I am not the man He thinks I am.

What if He called the wrong name.

Those questions do not shout. They speak softly, but they carry weight. They do not usually appear at the beginning of your journey, when enthusiasm is high and faith feels simple. They wait. They wait until obedience has cost you something. Until the miles behind you are as real as the miles ahead. Until the weight of responsibility settles into your bones and you realize there is no turning back without consequence.

They come after you have seen God move, and also watched things fall apart. After prayers were answered, and after others were not. After victories, and after moments that left you confused and tired. That is when the question finally steps out of the shadows and asks whether you really belong in this fight at all.

I know that moment. I have stood there myself more times than I want to admit. Moments when I wondered if I had misunderstood God, or overestimated what He placed inside me. Moments when it felt easier to believe I had misheard than to believe He was asking me to keep going.

But I am not the first.

The Bible is filled with men and women who trembled when God called their names. People who were living ordinary lives when Heaven interrupted them and placed something heavy in their hands. Responsibility they did not ask for. Callings they did not feel ready to carry.

And history is filled with the same. Men and women who woke up expecting another ordinary day and instead found themselves standing at the edge of something far bigger than they imagined.

Potential.

Hidden.

Untested.

Waiting.

That potential often stays buried until the moment God calls you into the dark. Because comfort rarely reveals what is inside you. Fear does. Pressure does. The unknown does.

And it is there, in the dark, that God begins to show you who He has always known you to be.

THE FARMER WHO BECAME A COMMANDER

There is a story from the old Roman Republic that has stayed with me for years: the story of Cincinnatus.

Plutarch records that when the Roman senators went looking for him, they did not find a man surrounded by influence or authority. They found him in a field.

Plutarch writes that they found Cincinnatus on his small farm, "either digging out a ditch or ploughing, at all events, as is generally agreed, intent on his husbandry."[*]

That detail matters to me.

Cincinnatus had led before. He had held authority before. He had been a soldier and a statesman. And then he had laid it down. Not in bitterness. Not in disgrace. He returned to ordinary life. To work that fed his family and demanded nothing from the public eye.

Then Rome fell into crisis.

An enemy army trapped Roman soldiers. Panic spread through the city. And the Senate did not look for someone campaigning to be in charge. They went back to the field. They interrupted a man who had learned how to be faithful without being seen.

Cincinnatus did not ask for the role.

He did not argue his qualifications.

He did not pretend to feel ready.

He wiped the dirt from his hands, handed the plow to his wife, and obeyed.

He led Rome to victory, restored order, and then did something almost unheard of. He resigned his authority and returned to his farm. He did not cling to power. He did not turn calling into identity. He completed the assignment and went back to the life entrusted to him.

Calling did not elevate him above others. It revealed who he already was.

God often calls people from places that look unimpressive. The field. The workshop. The quiet routines of faithfulness.

---

[*] Livy, *History of Rome*, translated by Rev. Canon Roberts, 3.26.6.

Calling rarely begins on a stage. It begins where obedience has already been practiced.

Hidden potential stays hidden until the call comes.

THE WOMAN WHO WALKED BACK INTO THE DARK

If Cincinnatus shows us the surprise of calling, Harriet Tubman shows us the cost.

Her life is one of the clearest pictures I know of someone walking directly into fear and discovering strength God had already placed inside her. She was born into slavery. Beaten. Scarred. Treated as property. Nothing in her circumstances suggested leadership or authority.

But God did not see her the way the world did.

When she escaped slavery and tasted freedom, she could have disappeared into safety. She could have protected the life she had barely managed to reclaim. Many would have understood if she had said, "I survived. That is enough."

But she heard another voice. A higher voice. The same voice that has unsettled Kingdom soldiers throughout history. The voice that does not merely rescue, but sends.

She said later, "To this solemn resolution I came; I was free, and they should be free also."[*]

That sentence carries weight. It is not idealism. It is obedience.

So she went back.

Not once. Again and again.

She walked hidden paths. She moved under cover of night. She led people who were terrified, wounded, and hunted. Fear

---

[*] Sarah Bradford, *Harriet: The Moses of Her People*. Geo R. Lockwood & Son, 1886, pg. 32.

did not disappear. But something else grew stronger. Discernment. Courage. Identity.

She did not wait to feel brave. She acted while afraid.

Like Gideon leaving the winepress.

Like Moses stepping back toward Pharaoh.

Like the disciples leaving their nets.

Calling did not create strength in her. It revealed it.

THE GIFT THAT WAS BURIED

Jesus tells a story that has always unsettled me.

A master prepares to leave on a journey and entrusts his servants with talents. Not symbols. Not small coins. Each talent represents enormous value. The master is not careless. He does not distribute scraps. He entrusts real wealth.

One servant receives five talents. Another receives two. A third receives one. Jesus is careful to say each was given "according to his ability" (Matthew 25:15). The master knew exactly what he was doing.

The first two servants act. They risk what they have been given. They put it to work. When the master returns, both have multiplied what was entrusted to them. Not equally, but faithfully.

Then there is the third servant.

He does not lose the talent.

He does not waste it.

He protects it.

He buries it.

And that is what makes the story uncomfortable.

The servant is not rebuked for recklessness. He is rebuked for fear. When the master returns, the servant explains himself simply.

"I was afraid."

Fear shapes his view of the master. Fear convinces him that

preservation is safer than obedience. Fear tells him the gift was too much, the risk too high, the calling misplaced.

I recognize that voice.

It whispers that God overestimated me. That He trusted me too much. That burying what He gave me is humility rather than avoidance.

Jesus exposes that lie.

The servant who buried his talent loses even what he has. Not because the master is cruel, but because potential that is never trusted is never transformed. Fear does not protect the gift. It suffocates it.

That is where Harriet Tubman stands in sharp contrast.

She could have buried what God placed in her. Trauma alone would have justified it. Danger made it reasonable. Freedom made it tempting. But she did not bury the gift. She placed it into motion.

Cincinnatus trusted the call and returned to obscurity when it was complete.

Tubman trusted the call and walked back into danger.

The faithful servants trusted the call and multiplied what they were given.

The only one who lost was the one who buried his gift.

That is the warning Jesus leaves us with. God does not give potential to be hidden. He gives it to be placed into motion. And the greatest danger is not failure. It is obedience delayed by fear.

THE CALL FORWARD

When I look back on my life, I can see moments when God placed something in my hands and said, *Do something with this.*

Not all at once. Not loudly. Often quietly. Sometimes without explanation.

A ministry assignment that felt heavier than my confidence.

A responsibility I knew mattered but did not feel ready to carry.

A step of obedience that unsettled me because it would cost something I could not get back.

In those moments, I did not feel heroic. I felt exposed.

I felt like the farmer standing at the plow, dirt still on his hands, wondering how an ordinary life suddenly became a summons. I felt like the woman weighing whether to step back into danger after tasting freedom. I felt like the servant staring at the talent in his hands, aware of its value and terrified of mishandling it.

Those moments were not dramatic on the outside. No thunder. No spotlight. Just an inner awareness that something had shifted and that staying where I was would no longer be honest.

Every soldier must face his cave.

Not the public battlefield. The private one. The place where excuses feel reasonable and fear sounds wise. The place where the question forms quietly: *What if God misjudged me?*

I have had to face that question more than once.

And over time, I have learned something that steadies me every time it returns.

God does not misjudge.

God does not miscalculate.

God does not call the wrong name.

The only real mistake is refusing to trust Him when He speaks.

THE HIDDEN POTENTIAL IN YOU

If you are honest, you feel it too.

Not ambition. Not restlessness for its own sake. Something quieter. A tension beneath the surface. A sense that there is more in you than what has been lived so far.

That feeling is easy to dismiss. Easy to spiritualize away or explain as dissatisfaction. But it keeps returning because it is not ego.

It is not pride.

It is not self-importance.

It is calling.

You are not a soldier because you trained yourself into one. You are a soldier because the King placed something inside you and expects it to be brought into the open. Calling does not always feel bold. Often it feels inconvenient. Heavy. Ill-timed.

God does not hand out talents to embarrass His servants. He hands them out to awaken them. To draw out what He already knows is there.

If God has placed something in your hands, it is not meant to be preserved in fear. It is meant to be trusted. Tested. Used. Not perfectly, but faithfully.

Hidden potential does not become purpose by waiting. It becomes purpose by obedience.

Cincinnatus returned to his field when his mission was complete.

Harriet Tubman kept walking into danger until as many as possible were free.

The faithful servants entered into the joy of their Master.

Different lives. Different assignments. Same pattern.

Obedience always produces a reward greater than fear.

This chapter is not meant to inspire you. It is meant to summon you.

Your name has been called.

Your potential is not buried.

It is waiting.

And the King is handing you your assignment.

EXERCISE: WHEN GOD CALLS YOUR NAME IN THE DARK

Before you move on from this chapter, I want to invite you into a quieter place. Every soldier needs moments like this. Not the classroom. Not the crowd. Not the battlefield. The cave.

The Bible is full of these moments. Gideon hiding in the winepress. David alone in the fields. Elijah in the cave. Jesus in the garden. These are the places where God speaks clearly, not because life is calm, but because distractions are removed.

So pause for a moment. Breathe. Let the noise settle.

I want you to think about the last time you sensed God putting something in your hands. It may not have felt dramatic. It may have felt inconvenient. A responsibility. A calling. A burden for someone else. A step of obedience you knew you were supposed to take but kept delaying.

Do not rush past this. Let the memory come.

Now ask yourself honestly: What did I do with what God gave me?

Did I step forward?

Did I hesitate?

Did I bury it under fear, doubt, or excuses?

There is no condemnation here. This is not a test. It is an invitation.

If you did not act, ask yourself why. What was the fear attached to it? Fear of failure. Fear of being seen. Fear of being wrong. Fear that God expected more from you than you could give.

Name that fear. Say it plainly. Fear loses power when it is brought into the light.

Now I want you to remember something important. God never hands out assignments casually. He never entrusts responsibility without provision. He never calls a man and then forgets to equip him. If He placed something in your hands, He did so on purpose.

Scripture says God gives gifts without regret. He does not change His mind about what He has placed inside you.

So ask Him a simple question:

"Lord, what do You want me to do with what You've given me right now?"

Do not overthink it. The first clear nudge matters.

Then ask Him for the courage to act, not someday, but today. Not when fear disappears. Not when you feel ready. Readiness often comes after obedience, not before it.

I want you to write two things down.

First, write what God has placed in your hands in this season. Be specific.

Second, write the fear that has kept you from acting.

When you are finished, pray this in your own words:

"Lord, I trust You more than my fear. I believe You did not misjudge me. Help me take the next step."

You do not have to leap. You just have to move.

A soldier is not defined by the absence of fear. He is formed by obedience in the presence of it.

When you are ready, stand up. Physically, if you can. Let that act mark something. You are not burying what God has given you. You are stepping forward with it.

Your potential is not buried.

It is awakening.

And the King is calling you forward.

10

VICTORY IN THE VALLEY

I have learned that every soldier eventually reaches a valley where the air is thin, the ground is uneven, and the shadows whisper that you will not make it. It is not a dramatic place. It does not announce itself. It simply appears, often after a season of obedience, when you least expect it. The strength you relied on feels diminished. The confidence you once carried feels heavier. Every step requires more effort than it used to.

What you do in that valley tells the truth about your faith. Valleys strip away borrowed strength. They remove the noise. They quiet the voices that once encouraged you. They leave you alone with what you actually believe. It does not matter how loudly you worship on the mountain if you abandon your post in the dark. Songs are easy when the view is clear. Standing is harder when you cannot see what lies ahead.

I have lived long enough to know that the valley is where real Kingdom Soldiers are forged. Not on parade grounds. Not when the music is playing. Not when the crowds cheer and obedience feels celebrated. We are formed in the spaces where our hearts break and our knees shake. In places where prayers feel unanswered. Where obedience costs something real. Where love feels like a risk instead of a reward. Where faith must be chosen without emotional reinforcement.

The valley always asks the same question. It does not shout. It whispers. It waits. Will you keep standing when it feels like God has stopped speaking?

That question reveals more than victory ever could.

DAVID RAN TOWARD HIS VALLEY

I still marvel at David, the shepherd boy who ran toward a giant while trained soldiers trembled. Everyone talks about the moment he slung the stone, but that is not the part that grips me. It is the running.

When the Philistine stepped forward, David sprinted. He did not wait for backup. He did not negotiate. He did not size up the danger. Something in him said, "This is the moment Heaven has been preparing me for." And he ran.

I know why he ran. The valley was calling. Destiny had stepped into the open. A soldier knows when God has pointed at an enemy and said, "This one is yours."

David's courage was not wild emotion. It was built in the secret places, back when he faced lions and bears with nothing but a staff and a prayer. God grows soldiers in quiet battles long before He unveils them in public.

Before there is ever a Goliath moment, there are a hundred small decisions no one sees. Those private victories matter. They build the spiritual muscle memory that lets you sprint toward giants on the day you are called.

You know those moments. The decision to kneel in prayer when the house is quiet. The decision to forgive when your flesh demands revenge. The decision to speak truth when everyone else has agreed to lie. These choices do not make headlines, but they make soldiers.

I picture young David in the wilderness, watching sheep, singing songs to God, learning to trust the Lord when no one was watching. He was not wasting time. He was training. He was building courage, one small obedience at a time. So when the giant mocked the armies of the living God, David did not hesitate. He had already been fighting battles in the dark. This one simply had an audience.

Faithfulness in the unseen prepares you for fruitfulness in the visible.

"I CANNOT COME DOWN"

Nehemiah's valley looked different. Instead of a giant, he faced distraction, threats, and taunts. Sanballat called him down off the wall again and again.

I can almost hear the voice. "Nehemiah, come down here. Just talk. Just stop building."

But Nehemiah answered like a soldier who understood his assignment.

"I am doing a great work, so that I cannot come down" (Nehemiah 6:3 KJV).

There have been seasons of my life when that one sentence carried me. Seasons when I felt the pull to abandon what God had asked of me. Seasons when grief whispered that obedience did not matter. Seasons when pain argued that the mission had changed. Seasons when exhaustion tried to convince me that God had forgotten my address.

But like Nehemiah, like David, like every nameless soldier who has stood their ground on a battlefield, I felt the Spirit steady my feet.

"Hold your post. You have a wall to build."

Some of you reading this are facing your own Sanballat. It may be a person. It may be a circumstance. It may be your own fear dressed up in reasonable arguments. And that voice keeps saying, "Come down. Step away. This is not worth it."

Do not listen.

Stay on your wall. Do the work God has given you. Let the mockers mock. Let the doubters doubt. You answer to a higher Commander.

Nehemiah did not have an easy assignment. His enemies surrounded him. His people were tired. The rubble was overwhelming. But he kept building. He armed his workers with swords in one hand and tools in the other. He prayed. He worked. And the wall went up.

That is what soldiers do. They hold the line. They do not wait for comfortable conditions. They serve in the conditions they are given.

CARMEN: A KINGDOM SOLDIER

My first wife, Carmen, my first love, fought a battle most people never saw and never understood. It was not public. It was not dramatic. There were no medals or applause. There were hospital rooms, long nights, and a slow, relentless wearing away of strength. She never carried a sword. Yet she faced her valley with a courage that still humbles me.

Scleroderma hardened her body, but her spirit never bent. Her frame weakened while her faith held. She sang when it hurt to breathe. She prayed when her voice could barely rise above a whisper. She endured suffering with a quiet dignity that still ministers to me years later. There was no bitterness in her. No demand for explanation. Only a steady trust that God was still God, even here.

Scleroderma tightens skin, muscles, and organs. It turns a body into a prison. Carmen watched her own strength slip away one painful day at a time. Tasks that were once simple became exhausting. Movements that once required no thought became deliberate and slow. Independence faded. Dependence grew. Yet she kept praising God. Not because she felt strong, but because she chose faith over fear again and again.

In the final months, her body weakened in ways that still bring tears to my eyes. Pain became constant. Breathing became work. Even smiling cost something. Yet she smiled for our children when she should have screamed in pain. She wanted them to remember her joy, not her suffering. She never cursed God. Never accused Him. Never stopped believing. She whispered worship songs when she no longer had the breath to sing them aloud.

I saw a soldier. Not one who charged forward, but one who stood firm. A warrior who held her post when retreat would have been easier. She did not fight loudly. She fought faithfully. She stood until the Commander called her home.

When she died on Valentine's Day, our son Isaac's twelfth birthday, in 1992, my heart shattered. Life split in two: before and after. She was able to enjoy the birthdays of our other two February children, Chamara and Ramone, just days prior. Those moments were gifts, sacred mercy in the middle of unbearable loss.

Afterward, I entered a valley darker than I imagined possible. Grief turned the lights out in my soul. Pain silenced my prayers. Scripture felt distant. Hope felt theoretical. I listened to lies I knew were lies, because they matched my pain. Lies that said the story was over. Lies that said the loss was final. Lies that said I was finished.

One night, I nearly ended my life behind the wheel. Speeding down Route 116, I closed my eyes and prepared to give in to despair. I wanted the pain to stop.

A semi roared past. Gravel shook the tires.

My eyes snapped open.

"Lord, I am sorry. Thank you for sparing my life. My kids need me."

The valley that nearly killed me became the valley where God rebuilt me. Slowly. Patiently. Gently. Not by removing the pain all at once, but by teaching me how to stand inside it without surrendering to it.

Carmen taught me faith in suffering. God taught me how to stand again. And the valley taught me something I have never forgotten.

Soldiers do not retire from their assignments simply because the battle hurts.

TUEY: A MODERN-DAY KINGDOM SOLDIER

When people meet my wife Tuey, they see strength and calm. They see quiet authority. They see steadiness. What they do not see is the fire she walked through before God restored her life. They see the fruit, but not the soil it grew out of. They see the confidence, but not the nights it was forged.

Her valley was not a single moment. It was a long season. A stretch of years marked by betrayal, heartbreak, and loneliness. Pain that did not come from her own choices, but from the brokenness of others. She carried wounds she did not deserve. And she carried them without becoming bitter.

Her first marriage, to my best friend Denzil, her first love, ended far too soon, after only two and a half years. Loss came quickly and without warning. Dreams ended abruptly. A future she had imagined vanished overnight. Yet in that darkest hour, she did not collapse. She grieved. She wept. She questioned. But she also found a reason to keep going.

She fought battles for her children while her own heart was breaking. She showed up when everything inside her wanted to disappear. She whispered prayers through tears that soaked pillows and floors. She got up on mornings when staying under the blankets felt like the only safe option. She chose faith when faith felt thin. She chose obedience when obedience felt costly.

There was no applause for that season. No recognition. No crowd cheering her endurance. There was only faith the size of a mustard seed. And she carried it faithfully. Day after day. Step after step. That kind of faith does not look impressive to the world, but Heaven notices it.

It was that faith that God honored. Not quickly. Not cheaply. But faithfully. And it was through that long obedience that she was blessed with a son, Xavier, at the age of forty-two. A gift that came not from comfort, but from perseverance. A reward that carried the fingerprints of God's timing and tenderness.

God carried her through. He rebuilt her from the inside out. He gave her a strength that did not come from ease, but from endurance. Not from being spared the valley, but from being faithful inside it. That is why her prayers carry weight. That is why her discernment is sharp. That is why her presence steadies a room. Valley-forged faith always does.

Tuey is living proof that your valley does not disqualify you. It trains you. It deepens you. It prepares you for influence you could never carry without it.

When I say I married a Kingdom Soldier, I mean it. She did not earn that title in a church service. She did not receive it from a platform. She earned it in the fire. In the nights when only God saw her tears. In the days when only grace kept her moving forward.

FORGED IN FIRE

Every soldier I admire has this in common: None were shaped by comfort. Not one of them was formed in ease, safety, or predictability. Comfort may soothe, but it does not strengthen.

Ease may preserve, but it does not prepare. Fire is what forges steel, and it is suffering that forges soldiers.

David grew in fields and caves, learning to trust God when no one was watching and no one was applauding. Nehemiah grew under pressure and threats, building with one hand while holding a weapon in the other. Cincinnatus grew behind a plow, faithful in obscurity long before history ever called his name. Harriet Tubman grew under chains, discovering courage where most would have surrendered to despair. Carmen grew under pain that crushed her body but could not bend her spirit. Tuey grew in a valley of betrayal and hardship, where faith had to be chosen daily, sometimes hourly, without any visible reward.

I grew in a valley I never asked for. One I would have avoided if given the choice. One that stripped me of illusions I did not know I was clinging to. It dismantled the version of faith I had built on comfort and replaced it with something truer, heavier, and more resilient.

That valley is where God forged my message. Not in theory. Not in sermons. But in tears, questions, and long nights where obedience was the only thing left to cling to. The battles that break us often become the stories that heal others. The wounds we survive become the places through which grace flows most freely. Your mess becomes your message when you surrender it to the King and stop trying to manage it on your own.

I would not choose my valley again. I would not romanticize it. I would not wish it on anyone I love. But I would not trade what God gave me there. In that darkness, I found His light, not as an idea but as a presence. In that weakness, I found His strength, not as a slogan but as sustenance. In that death, I tasted resurrection, not someday, but now.

Nothing is wasted in God's hands. Not pain. Not loss. Not suffering. Not even the valleys we wish had never existed.

When surrendered to Him, every fire becomes a forge, and every valley becomes holy ground.

YOUR VALLEY IS NOT THE END

Maybe you are in a valley right now. Maybe the air feels thin and every step takes more effort than it should. Maybe your hope is tired, not gone, just worn down from carrying unanswered prayers for too long. Maybe you have prayed for forty days or forty years and nothing seems to have shifted.

Hear me.

If God has allowed you to walk into a valley, He will give you what you need to walk out of it. He does not lead His soldiers into terrain He has not already accounted for. He does not abandon His own in the places where the cost is highest. Valleys are not evidence of His absence. They are often evidence of His purpose.

You are not alone, even when it feels like no one can reach you. You are not forgotten, even when heaven feels quiet. You are not too broken to be used, even when your own strength feels spent. Your valley is not a punishment. It is a training ground. A place where God strips away what cannot survive the next season and strengthens what must.

And your story will become a lifeline for someone else. Not because you have the right words, but because you stayed. Because you endured. Because you kept walking when it would have been easier to sit down and give up. Someone will recognize their own pain in yours and realize survival is possible.

Soldiers do not hide scars. Scars are not shame. They are proof. Proof that the enemy struck and failed. Proof that you stayed in the fight. Proof that God carried you through what should have destroyed you.

The world does not need polished testimonies or carefully edited victories. The world needs soldiers who have been through fire and still believe. Men and women who can say, without exaggeration or denial, "I did not escape the valley unchanged, but I did not lose my faith there, either."

Your valley is not the end of your story.

It is the place where endurance is formed, authority is earned, and hope becomes unshakeable.

YOUR ASSIGNMENT THIS WEEK

Before this chapter ends, I want you to do one thing.

Tell one person your story.

Not the edited version. The real one.

Someone needs what God forged in your valley. Someone is standing where you once stood. Someone is waiting for a soldier to say, "I have been there. Here is how God brought me through."

Your testimony is a weapon. A lifeline. A holy gift.

The enemy wants to silence it. Do not let him.

Soldiers do not retreat.

They advance.

PART IV

THE KINGDOM ADVANCE

11

SPECIAL FORCES TRAINING

I have always been fascinated by the men who choose hard paths on purpose. Not because they want to be noticed, but because the mission demands a certain kind of person. During World War Two, long before America had Navy SEALs or Green Berets, there was a unit formed in secrecy, trained in silence, and deployed behind enemy lines. They were called the Office of Strategic Services, the OSS. Most people today have never heard of them, but they were the fathers of our modern Special Forces.

The OSS did not recruit the strongest. They recruited the ones who could endure. Bankers, farmers, college athletes, linguists, loggers, professors, mechanics, missionaries. Men who looked ordinary on the outside but carried something uncommon within them. Their training was brutal. They learned to survive with almost nothing. They were pushed past exhaustion and into the hidden places of their will. Instructors studied how a man responded when sleep-deprived, hungry, cold, or afraid. They wanted to see if he would fold or if he would fight.

One OSS trainer put it this way: "We are looking for men

who can operate alone, behind enemy lines, without losing their mission, their mind, or their moral compass." In other words, they needed soldiers who would hold steady in the dark, without applause, without comfort, and often without support. Soldiers whose discipline would keep them alive when everything else around them fell apart.

The OSS did not fight in the open. They slipped in through cracks in the world. Behind the noise of the battlefield, they sabotaged enemy supply lines, coordinated with local resistance forces, rescued prisoners, and gathered intelligence that saved thousands of lives. And almost no one ever knew their names. They did their work in silence so that others could live in freedom.

When I think about the next level of spiritual training, this is the picture that comes to mind. Not the polished Christian life that looks good on Sunday, but the hidden life that is forged under pressure. The life God builds when no one is watching. The kind of soldier who does not need applause to stay faithful. The kind who will follow orders in the dark because he has already surrendered everything in the light.

Special Forces soldiers are not made on the battlefield. They are made in training. The battle only reveals what the training already built. And the same is true in the Kingdom. Anyone can shout on the mountaintop, but only a trained soldier stands firm in the valley. God prepares His elite warriors in private long before they ever step into public assignments. He strengthens, purifies, and breaks us down to build us up. Not to shame us, but to sharpen us. Not to weaken us, but to make us reliable under fire.

I believe the Lord has always had His own version of Special Forces. Men and women hidden in prayer. Intercessors who stand in the gap. Evangelists who go where others will not. Servants who labor in quiet faithfulness. Disciples who endure temptation without folding. Believers who walk in such discipline and devotion that when the enemy pushes, they do not move.

This chapter is about that kind of training. Not basic training. Not the first steps of faith. Not the early lessons of the battlefield. This is the advanced course. The kind of training where the Lord takes you beyond comfort and into calling. Where He develops the spiritual muscles you do not get from casual Christianity. Where obedience becomes instinct. Where prayer becomes air. Where the Word becomes your true weapon. And where your loyalty to the Commander is not based on blessings, but on covenant.

Just as the OSS trained warriors who could operate behind enemy lines, God trains Kingdom Soldiers to move with wisdom, discipline, and courage in a world that is dark and often hostile to the truth. Soldiers who can think clearly under pressure. Soldiers who do not panic when the enemy roars. Soldiers who know how to advance the mission even when they stand alone. Soldiers who have been shaped by the Holy Spirit into men and women who can endure hardship as good soldiers of Jesus Christ.

If you are reading this chapter, it may be because the Lord is calling you into the deeper waters. Not everyone is ready for this level of training. But every believer is invited. Jesus is not looking for perfect people. He is looking for willing ones. Those who will let Him refine them the way a Special Forces instructor refines a recruit: with purpose, with love, and with a vision of who they can become.

You do not rise to the occasion in the Kingdom. You fall to the level of your training. And now, the Holy Spirit is ready to take you deeper.

BIBLICAL SPECIAL FORCES: DAVID'S MIGHTY MEN

And this kind of training is not new. Long before modern armies, long before the OSS slipped behind enemy lines in Europe, God Himself raised up a group of elite warriors. They were not known for perfect backgrounds or elite pedigree. They were known for loyalty, courage, and the ability to keep fighting when ordinary men would have walked away. Scripture calls them David's Mighty Men.

They did not become mighty on the battlefield. They became mighty in the wilderness under David's leadership, long before he sat on the throne. These were men shaped in caves, not palaces. They were forged while running from Saul, not while sitting in victory. They learned obedience through hardship, brotherhood through suffering, and courage through the repeated process of trusting God when the odds were impossible.

One of them lifted his spear against eight hundred enemies and still stood at the end. Another fought until his hand froze to his sword, refusing to let go even as his strength ran out. Another defended a field of lentils while everyone else retreated. And three of them once broke through an entire Philistine garrison just to bring their king a drink of water from Bethlehem's well. Not because David ordered it. Because love compelled them.

What made these men mighty was not that they were fearless. It was that fear never dictated their loyalty. They understood the heart of their king. They embraced the costs that others avoided. They trained in obscurity. They learned to hear a command even when it was whispered, and they executed it with precision and honor. And long before anyone else called them mighty, God did.

Every generation has its Mighty Men. Its OSS warriors. Its

hidden ones. And I believe the Lord is calling many of us into that same kind of training today. Not the shallow kind. Not the casual kind. The kind that forms spiritual instincts. The kind that builds a soldier who will not break in the dark. The kind that turns a believer into someone God can trust with assignments that require grit and endurance.

Special Forces training in the Kingdom is not about becoming more important. It is about becoming more surrendered. It is learning to live with the kind of discipline that keeps you steady when the battle shifts. It is the quiet decision to say yes to God when no one is watching. It is the willingness to let Him take you deeper into prayer, deeper into His Word, deeper into obedience, deeper into repentance, deeper into worship, deeper into spiritual maturity. It is what separates the spectators from the soldiers.

When God begins this kind of training, He usually starts in the hidden places. He teaches you to recognize His voice when distractions are loud. He trains your heart to obey quickly even when the assignment does not make sense. He strengthens you to stand firm when life pushes hard. He bends your will until it aligns with His, and He does it not to crush you, but to make you unshakable. Because He knows the battles ahead. He knows the assignments coming. And He knows what kind of soldier you must become to complete them.

This is where many believers stop. They want the armor, but not the weight of it. They want the victory cries, but not the training hours. They want the anointing of David without the wilderness of David. They want the authority of a Mighty Man without the discipline that made them mighty. But the battlefield will not accept shortcuts. The moment spiritual pressure hits, a soldier will always fall to the level of his training. Always.

So the Lord draws us into Special Forces training. He invites us to become people who can carry weight in the Kingdom without collapsing. People who can stand in places others avoid. People who can walk into spiritual situations that require discernment, endurance, courage, and unwavering faith. People whose loyalty to the King is not seasonal, emotional, or fragile but anchored in covenant.

I have learned that this kind of training is not glamorous. It is not posted online. It is not applauded. It is often lonely, stretching, inconvenient, and uncomfortable. But it is the place where strength is born. It is the place where character is shaped. It is the place where God's voice becomes clear and your identity as a soldier becomes firm. And once you have walked through this kind of training, you carry something inside you that the enemy cannot easily shake loose.

Just like the OSS, just like David's Mighty Men, God is still forming Kingdom Soldiers who can carry out His mission with wisdom and courage. Soldiers who are not intimidated by obstacles. Soldiers who know how to fight and how to stand. Soldiers who can hold the line even when darkness presses hard. Soldiers who understand that the deeper the training, the greater the trust the Commander places on them.

FORGED IN THE HIDDEN PLACES

Special Forces training always begins in hidden places. Before a man ever parachuted behind enemy lines, he learned discipline in obscurity. Before he carried a mission file, he carried a pack in the mud. Before he mastered strategy, he mastered obedience. And before he walked in authority, he learned to walk in submission.

The Kingdom is no different.

My private battles became my training ground. My prayers became my conditioning. The Word became my weapon. Worship became my breath. Fasting became the discipline that told my flesh it was no longer in charge. The Holy Spirit became the Instructor who did not flatter me but shaped me.

He corrected me, refined me, tested me, and strengthened me for assignments I could not yet see.

There were nights I asked God, "Why is this so hard?" And the Lord would answer, sometimes gently, sometimes firmly: "Because comfort will not prepare you for the mission I am giving you."

Every hardship was building endurance. Every delay was sharpening discernment. Every unanswered question was teaching trust. Every spiritual attack was forming spiritual muscle.

And then one day, something shifted. The training that once felt heavy began to feel like purpose. The battles that once overwhelmed me became opportunities to draw closer to the Commander. The Word was not just something I read; it became the voice that steadied my steps. Prayer was not merely communication; it was strategy. And obedience became the greatest expression of love.

This is the difference between a believer who attends church and a believer who has been trained. One can quote verses. The other can wield them. One can sing about faith. The other can stand in it. One can talk about the battle. The other can survive it.

Kingdom Special Forces are not made by titles, positions, or personality. They are shaped in the hidden, quiet, demanding places where the Holy Spirit trains a soul to endure.

Just as the OSS sent its men behind enemy lines to rescue captives, the Lord sends His soldiers into spiritual darkness to bring light, truth, and freedom. This is our Great Commission. Not optional. Not negotiable. A direct assignment from the Commander.

Some missions will look simple. A conversation. A prayer. A moment of encouragement. Some will cost you comfort, pride, or security. Some will send you into places others avoid. But every assignment comes from the same authority. And every assignment is sacred.

If you want to be used by God at this level, you must allow Him to train you at this level.

You cannot carry a Special Forces assignment with a casual faith. You cannot endure the front line with an untrained spirit. And you cannot fight spiritual battles with a heart that refuses discipline.

God is not training you for a playground. He is preparing you for warfare. He is shaping you for missions He has written into your destiny. And the time you spend with Him now is the strength you will stand in later.

WHAT KINGDOM SPECIAL FORCES TRAINING LOOKS LIKE

When God begins to train you at this level, it does not feel glamorous. It feels costly. The Spirit takes you past basic training and draws you into a deeper, narrower path. He begins to shape you in ways that ordinary believers will never fully understand, because He is preparing you for assignments that require more than enthusiasm. They require maturity.

The first thing God does is intensify your **prayer life.** Not your routine prayers, but the prayers that expose your heart. The prayers that reach into the deep places you would rather avoid. The prayers that demand honesty. When the Holy Spirit pulls you into this place, He is not teaching you to pray prettier; He is teaching you to pray with authority. He is giving you a spiritual ear for the Father's voice and a spiritual gut for the weight of His burden. You begin to pray differently because you begin to see differently.

Then the Lord deepens your relationship with **His Word.** Not as a devotion you check off, but as your lifeline. You start to sense the weight of Scripture, how it slices through confusion, how it exposes lies, how it steadies your heart. The Word becomes more than a book; it becomes a weapon placed in your hands by your Commander. You start to store it in your heart, not to show off your knowledge, but so that when the enemy whispers, you can answer with truth without hesitation.

God also trains you in **obedience**, and this is where many soldiers fall off the path. Obedience means responding to God even when you are tired, when you are unsure, when the timing seems wrong, when the cost seems high. Special Forces soldiers are not impressive because of strength; they are impressive because of submission. They have learned the discipline of listening. That same discipline is what the Holy Spirit develops in you. He teaches you to move when He says move and to stand still when He says wait. Both are equally important, and neither comes naturally.

The Lord will also begin to teach you to **discipline** your flesh. Not for punishment, but for clarity. Fasting becomes part of your life, not a ritual, but a way to silence the noise inside you so you can hear the voice above you. You learn to say no to cravings that weaken your focus. You learn to separate yourself from old habits that drain your strength. You learn that freedom is not doing what you want. Freedom is being able to obey when God speaks.

Another part of the training is **endurance**. The Holy Spirit will allow you to walk through seasons where you cannot see results right away. You pray, and the answer does not come quickly. You serve, and no one applauds. You obey, and the door stays shut. He is not ignoring you. He is stretching you. He is teaching you that spiritual strength is not measured by immediate outcomes, but by long-term faithfulness.

Pressure has a way of revealing whether your foundation is built on emotion or commitment. Many believers quit because they think delay means denial. But a soldier learns early that delay is part of the mission. It is a test of whether you will remain loyal when God seems silent.

God also trains you to stay **focused**. Special Forces soldiers do not get wrapped up in civilian distractions. They live on mission. The same is true for you. There comes a point where the Spirit begins to strip away unnecessary weight. He cuts loose relationships that pull you off course. He exposes patterns that keep you unfocused. He shines light on habits you thought were harmless but were slowing you down. Purpose requires pruning. And pruning always comes before power.

And as you grow, God places you in **community**, because no soldier is trained alone. He places people around you who challenge you, correct you, and sharpen you. Some believers resist this part because accountability feels uncomfortable. But isolation is dangerous. A lone soldier becomes an easy target. The army of God is built on unity, not independence. The Holy Spirit trains you to fight with your brothers and sisters, not apart from them.

Then comes the hardest training of all: **suffering**. Not suffering for suffering's sake, but suffering that teaches you to trust God beyond logic. These are the seasons where faith is stripped down to its core. Seasons where you pray through tears. Seasons where obedience feels painful. Seasons where you are forced to depend on God for every step. This is where the strongest soldiers are shaped. Not in victories, but in valleys.

When this work is done in you, something changes. You are no longer tossed around by emotion. You are steadied by conviction. You are no longer intimidated by resistance. You are strengthened by experience. You are no longer hesitant when God speaks. You are trained to respond.

A Kingdom Soldier who has undergone Special Forces training walks with a different posture. They are not louder. They are deeper. They do not run from battle. They recognize it and step into it with confidence in the One who trained them. They do not serve for applause. They serve because the Commander assigned them.

And most importantly, *they know who they belong to.*

A soldier who has been trained at this level does not confuse who they fight for, who they answer to, or who sustains them. Their allegiance is settled. Their loyalty is anchored. Their heart is aligned. Their mind is renewed. Their spirit is fortified.

This is the work the Holy Spirit does in every believer who is willing. And the moment you accept this training, Heaven sees you differently.

You are no longer a spectator. You are a soldier. You are no longer on the sidelines. You are in formation. You are no longer waiting for purpose. You are walking in it.

THE TRAINING THAT SHAPES YOU

The OSS and David's Mighty Men show us a simple truth: Before God entrusts a soldier with a dangerous mission, He first builds someone who can carry it. He shapes them in quiet places, tests them in hidden ones, and strengthens them in difficult ones. No one wakes up a Special Forces soldier. They are formed in fire.

That is why the men who served under David did not become mighty because they were naturally impressive. They became mighty because they learned to follow their king in caves before they followed him in victory. They learned loyalty when no one applauded them. They learned obedience when the world misunderstood them. These men were not pampered. They were proven.

In my own walk, I have discovered that God trains His soldiers the same way. Before He puts you in a place where others are depending on your strength, He will put you in a place where only He can strengthen you. Before He uses your voice publicly, He refines your heart privately. Before He trusts you with influence, He tests you in fidelity. Before He sends you into darkness, He teaches you how to stand in the light.

This is the training that separates Kingdom Special Forces from casual believers. Not rank. Not status. Not talent. But surrender.

The soldiers in the OSS learned quickly that comfort was not a right. It was a distraction. They learned to crawl through mud, run in cold and heat, and push their bodies to the edge. What mattered was not who finished first but who refused to quit. Those who quit were never shamed. They simply could not carry the mission. Pressure revealed the difference.

God uses pressure the same way. He uses trials to toughen your faith. He uses delays to strengthen your patience. He uses disappointment to anchor your identity. He uses spiritual resistance to train your discernment. None of this is punishment. All of it is preparation.

Some lessons you will not learn from sermons. You learn them in battles you did not expect. Some prayers you will not pray until you are backed into a corner. Some strength you will not discover until your heart has been pushed past its own limits. Some obedience you will not practice until the Lord asks you to do what your flesh resists.

When you walk with God long enough, you eventually understand why the Holy Spirit trains you so intensely. The battles ahead require more than knowledge. They require endurance. They require clarity. They require discipline. They require a heart that listens instantly to the Commander's voice.

This is why the Spirit confronts you, corrects you, and shapes you. He is your Instructor. Not working against you, but working through you. Teaching you how to obey. Teaching you how to pray. Teaching you how to hear. Teaching you how to stand. Teaching you how to endure.

A soldier does not succeed because of raw strength. He succeeds because obedience becomes instinct. He succeeds because he learned his Commander's voice. He succeeds because the training has become part of him. And when fear rises, training speaks louder.

The same is true for every Kingdom Soldier. When temptation comes, you stand if you have trained. When storms hit, you endure if you have trained. When spiritual resistance arrives, you discern if you have trained. When life shakes you, you remain unbroken if your roots go deep.

This is why I tell believers that God does not waste a single hardship. Every hardship is shaping something eternal in you. Every disappointment is building dependence. Every tear is teaching trust. Every moment of resistance is strengthening your spiritual muscles. None of this is random. It is all part of your training.

The OSS trained men to go behind enemy lines. The Lord trains His soldiers to go behind spiritual ones. To rescue the lost. To speak truth into darkness. To break generational patterns. To carry light where there is despair. To fight for families, churches, communities, and destinies. To stand where others fold.

When the Holy Spirit begins this work in you, expect to be stretched. Expect to be challenged. Expect to be refined. Expect to be made strong in places you were once fragile. Expect your appetite to change. Expect your focus to sharpen. Expect your vision to widen. Expect your courage to grow. This is what happens when God begins to train a soldier.

And when that training goes deep, something beautiful happens. You discover that you were not made for ordinary assignments. You were made for obedience. You were made for endurance. You were made for spiritual authority. You were made for a mission. You were made to carry the heart of your King into places where others cannot go.

This is the Kingdom Special Forces: Believers who have learned to take orders from the Spirit. Believers who have let God break them so He can rebuild them. Believers who know who they are, who their Commander is, and what their mission requires. Believers who advance the Kingdom with clarity, courage, and love. Believers who carry assignments that matter in eternity.

KINGDOM SPECIAL FORCES TRAINING GUIDE

If you sense that God is calling you beyond basic training, this is how you begin. This is not a quick fix or a spiritual fad. It is a way of life. Think of this as your first phase of Kingdom Special Forces training.

I encourage you to commit to this for at least thirty days.

Step 1: Report for Duty Every Morning

A soldier does not wander into the day. He reports.

Each morning, before you check your phone, turn on the news, or start your schedule, present yourself to your Commander.

Pray something like this: "Lord Jesus, I report for duty today. I belong to You. My mind, my body, my time, and my assignments are Yours. Give me my orders and the grace to obey."

Sit quietly for a few moments. Let your heart settle. You are not just waking up. You are checking in.

Set a specific wakeup time you can keep. Even if you only have fifteen minutes, give the first portion of your day to the Lord as your reporting time.

Step 2: Establish a Daily Word Watch

Special Forces soldiers do not wait until they are in a firefight to learn how to use their weapon. They train with it daily until it feels natural in their hands.

Your weapon is the Word of God.

Choose a focused section of Scripture for this training season. It might be Ephesians 6, 2 Timothy 2, the Psalms, the Gospels, or another book the Spirit has highlighted to you.

Each day, read a portion slowly. Ask yourself what God is showing you about Himself, about you, and about the battle you are in. Write one verse, phrase, or truth that you will carry into your day.

Commit to a minimum of one chapter or a clearly defined passage each day. Do not rush. This is not about volume. It is about depth.

Step 3: Build a Real Prayer Block

This is where God shifts you from casual praying to strategic communion.

Set a daily prayer block. Start with fifteen minutes if needed, and let it grow. Use that time to worship God for who He is, confess anything that is hindering your walk, pray for strength, wisdom, and purity, and intercede for specific people and situations God has put on your heart.

Picture it as your briefing with Headquarters. You are not reciting lines. You are receiving instructions.

Choose a fixed time and place. Guard that block like an appointment with your commanding officer. If you miss it, you feel it.

Step 4: Introduce a Weekly Fast

Special Forces training teaches a soldier to say no to his own comfort. Fasting trains your spirit to lead and your flesh to follow.

Choose one approach you can sustain. Skip one meal once or twice a week and use that time to pray. Or fast from something that has a strong pull on you, such as social media, entertainment, or certain foods, for a set period.

During that fast, make it a point to seek God's face, not just His hand. Ask Him to purify your motives, sharpen your hearing, and strengthen your will.

Pick one regular day as your training day for fasting. Start small, stay consistent, and let God deepen it.

Step 5: Practice Immediate Obedience

This is where everything shifts.

Special Forces soldiers are trusted because they have learned to respond quickly. They do not debate every order. They do not negotiate every instruction. They have trained themselves to move.

Ask the Lord each day: "What is one thing You are asking me to obey today?"

It might be forgiving someone, making a phone call, starting a conversation, giving something away, turning off something that is pulling you down, or stepping out to serve.

When you sense that nudge, do not postpone it. Obedience delayed becomes obedience denied.

Write down one concrete act of obedience each day, then do it before you go to bed that night.

Step 6: Embrace an Endurance Assignment

Special Forces training includes long marches, repeated drills, and demanding conditions. It is not about speed. It is about stamina.

Ask the Lord for one endurance assignment in this season. Something that will stretch you beyond convenience. It might be committing to a consistent place of serving in your church, walking with a new believer for three months, showing up weekly to a prayer meeting or small group, or visiting a shut-in, a prison ministry, or a neighborhood outreach regularly.

There will be days when you do not feel like continuing. That is exactly when the training is doing its deepest work.

Name your endurance assignment and share it with a trusted believer so they can hold you accountable.

Step 7: Join or Strengthen Your Unit

No Special Forces soldier fights alone. They train, move, and operate as a team.

If you are not in a small group, prayer circle, or discipleship group, this is part of your training. If you are already in one, this is where you lean in, not check out.

Show up consistently. Share honestly. Pray for one another. Be willing to be challenged and corrected in love. Let iron sharpen iron.

Commit to at least one regular gathering with other believers where the focus is growth, not entertainment. Treat that time as part of your training orders, not an optional social event.

Step 8: Face a Fear With God

Every soldier has fears. Special Forces training does not pretend they do not exist. It teaches them to move through fear with confidence in their training and their commander.

Ask the Holy Spirit to put His finger on one fear that has been holding you back. It might be fear of rejection, fear of failure, fear of sharing your faith, or fear of stepping into a new calling.

Then, with God's help, take one concrete step against that fear. Have the conversation. Apply for the position. Share your testimony with one person. Volunteer where you feel unqualified. Let God meet you on the other side of obedience.

Once a week, do one specific thing that you could not see yourself doing six months ago. Journal afterward what God showed you.

Step 9: Debrief With the Lord

Special Forces teams debrief after missions. They do not just move on. They review, learn, and adjust.

Set aside time once a week to sit with the Lord and ask: "What victories did You give me this week? Where did I miss You or resist You? What are You saying to me for the coming week?"

Write down what He shows you. Celebrate progress, confess where you pulled back, and ask for fresh grace. This keeps your training sharp and your heart humble.

Have a consistent debrief day with the Lord. It might be Sunday afternoon or another quiet window. Treat it as part of your ongoing training.

Step 10: Renew Your Oath

A Special Forces soldier does not forget who he serves. Every so often, he comes back to his oath.

As a Kingdom Soldier, you do the same.

Regularly say to the Lord: "I belong to You. I am not my own. I have been bought with a price. I am here to please my Commander and finish the assignment You have given me."

This settles your heart when the battle is long and the path is narrow.

When you feel tired, misunderstood, or tempted to quit, renew your oath. Say it out loud. Stand on it. Let it remind you that you are not a volunteer. You are enlisted.

THE SOLDIER YOU ARE BECOMING

And now that you have seen the purpose of the training and you have been given the steps to begin, let me speak directly to you.

This training is not for everyone. Not because God plays favorites, but because not everyone is willing. Some believers want comfort more than calling. Some want blessings more than obedience. Some want to be celebrated more than they want to be faithful. And that is their choice.

But you are still reading. That tells me something. It tells me that there is something inside you that refuses to settle. Something that hears the Commander's voice and wants to respond. Something that knows there is more to this life than playing it safe and hoping you make it to Heaven.

You were made for more. You were made to be trained. You were made to be trusted. You were made to carry assignments that matter in eternity. You were made to stand where others fall. You were made to advance the Kingdom.

And the moment you say yes to this training, something

shifts in the spirit realm. Heaven takes notice. The Commander writes your name in a different column. You are no longer waiting for your life to begin. You are walking into it.

Because every Kingdom Soldier reaches a moment where the Spirit whispers: "You are ready for the next level."

And this is where the real training begins.

12

RESURRECTION POWER

LIVING FROM VICTORY, NOT FOR VICTORY

Earlier, in chapter 3, we looked at David to confront the lie of insignificance. We saw him as the unlikely choice, the overlooked shepherd, the proof that God delights in using "just one person" to accomplish what armies cannot. That story was about calling. It was about permission. It was about silencing the voice that says you are too small to matter.

Now I want you to see David through a different lens.

This time, David is not here to convince you that God can use you. He is here to show you how a Kingdom Soldier thinks and moves once the call has already been accepted. This is no longer about whether God can use one person. It is about how that person stands when fear freezes everyone else.

David's victory over Goliath was not an impulsive act of courage. It was the fruit of long, unseen formation. Fields before battlefields. Lions and bears before giants. Worship before warfare. Faith forged in obscurity before faith displayed in public.

In other words, David did not become brave in the valley of Elah. He arrived brave.

That is why we return to his story. Not to repeat the miracle, but to study the mindset. Not to re-prove God's power, but to understand how a trained heart responds under pressure. Not to ask, "Can God use someone like me?" but to answer a harder question: "How do I stand when it is my turn to run toward the giant?"

This is where calling becomes training and training becomes action.

When David ran toward Goliath, he was not a fool rushing to his death. He was a young man who understood something the trained soldiers around him had forgotten.

He knew he was not fighting for victory. He was fighting from it.

Scripture tells us exactly what David said to the Philistine giant:

Then said David to the Philistine, Thou comest to me with a sword, and with a spear, and with a shield: but I come to thee in the name of the LORD of hosts, the God of the armies of Israel, whom thou hast defied...and all this assembly shall know that the LORD saveth not with sword and spear: for the battle is the LORD's, and He will give you into our hands.

— 1 SAMUEL 17:45, 47 KJV

For forty days Goliath had mocked the armies of Israel. Grown men who were trained for war stayed in the trenches, listening to the threats of one giant. Every morning and every evening, he taunted them, and every day, they chose fear over faith. They had the armor. They had the numbers. They had the God of Abraham, Isaac, and Jacob on their side. But they stood paralyzed while one loud voice told them they could not win.

Then David arrived, sent by his father on a simple errand.

Jesse told him to take food to his brothers and bring back a report. David did not wake up that morning planning to face a giant. He woke up planning to deliver bread and cheese.

Instead, he walked into a divine setup.

I have learned over the years that God often works this way. He positions you for an assignment before you even know there is one. You think you are just going about your day, doing something ordinary, and then suddenly you are standing in the middle of a moment that will define your faith. David was not looking for Goliath. God was looking for David.

David listened to Goliath's insults and watched the soldiers scatter. Something rose up in him. He said, "Who is this uncircumcised Philistine, that he should defy the armies of the living God?" (1 Samuel 17:26 KJV). And when his own brothers tried to silence him, when they accused him of pride and curiosity, his answer was simple and profound: "What have I now done? Is there not a cause?" (1 Samuel 17:29 KJV).

That question still echoes through history.

Is there not a cause?

That is resurrection power in the heart of a Kingdom Soldier. It is not arrogance. It is not hype. It is not the bravado of someone who does not understand what he is facing. It is a settled conviction that our God is greater than any giant, and that the battle belongs to Him.

David did not minimize the threat. He acknowledged that Goliath was big, armed, and dangerous. But he also knew something the other soldiers had forgotten. He knew that the God who had delivered him from the lion and the bear would deliver him from this Philistine. He knew that the battle was not ultimately about his strength or skill; it was about the name and the honor of the living God.

And so he ran.

Not away from the giant. Toward him.

THE GOD FACTOR

As believers, we must take a serious look at what is happening around us. The devil is daily taking loved ones, friends, neighbors, and someone else's precious family members captive.

Paul wrote to Timothy about this spiritual reality: "...and they may come to their senses and escape from the snare of the devil, after being captured by him to do his will" (2 Timothy 2:26).

This is not figurative language. This is not religious poetry. This is the condition of millions of people walking around in bondage to an enemy they cannot see and often do not even believe exists. They are trapped in addiction, despair, bitterness, and confusion. They are living under the weight of lies they think are truth. And they do not know there is a way out.

David understood that his battle was more than a single fight. If the Philistines won that day, entire families would be taken captive. Futures would be stolen. Men would be eliminated as future threats. Women and children would be carried off into slavery. One boy's obedience on that battlefield affected generations.

The same is true today.

When you stand in your God-given authority, you are not just standing for yourself. You are standing for your family, your children, your grandchildren, your church, and often for people you may never meet on this side of eternity. Your courage matters. Your faith matters. Your obedience matters. Because the battles you fight in the spiritual realm have consequences in the natural realm that ripple out further than you can imagine.

That is why we cannot live our Christian lives in the trenches.

Too many believers have made the trenches their address. Always on the defensive. Always hiding. Always hoping the enemy will leave them alone. Always waiting for someone else to do the fighting.

But God is raising an army of Kingdom Soldiers who will not stay in the trench. People who understand that the Cross has already decided the outcome. People who know that Jesus did not die just so we could survive. He died so we could advance.

Paul wrote to the Colossians about what happened at the Cross: "He disarmed the rulers and authorities and put them to open shame, by triumphing over them in him" (Colossians 2:15).

And John wrote to believers facing spiritual opposition: "Little children, you are from God and have overcome them, for he who is in you is greater than he who is in the world" (1 John 4:4).

We do not fight for victory. We fight from it.

The victory has already been won. The outcome has already been decided. The enemy has already been disarmed and publicly shamed. What remains is for us to walk in what Christ has already accomplished, to enforce on earth what Heaven has already declared.

THE FINISHED WORK OF THE CROSS

On the Cross, Jesus did not almost win. He did not put in a good effort and then hand the rest of the work to us. He did not get halfway there and say, "Now it is up to you to finish what I started."

He finished it.

His final words from the Cross were not a cry of defeat. They were a declaration of completion. "It is finished." The Greek word is *tetelestai*. It was a word used in commerce to mark a debt as paid in full. When Jesus said it, He was announcing to Heaven, earth, and hell that the price had been paid. The debt was settled. The work was done.

He took our sin, our guilt, and our shame. He satisfied the justice of God. He broke the power of death. He disarmed the rulers and authorities of darkness. He opened the way for us to be reconciled to the Father. He did what no human being could ever do for themselves.

Then He rose.

The resurrection is not an afterthought to the Gospel. It is the exclamation point. It is the proof that everything Jesus said and did was true. It is the demonstration that death itself could not hold Him, that the grave could not keep Him, that the enemy's greatest weapon had been turned into a trophy.

Resurrection power means the victory of Jesus is not just a story we tell. It is a reality we live in.

We are justified by grace, not by performance. We are accepted in the Beloved, not tolerated on probation. We are adopted as sons and daughters, not hired as servants trying to earn a wage. We are not on trial. We are not under condemnation. We are not waiting to find out if we made the cut.

We are in Christ. And in Christ, we are more than conquerors.

The Gospel of Grace is not a soft gospel. It is not a weak gospel for people who cannot handle the truth. It is the Gospel of a King who conquered sin, death, hell, and the grave, and then said, "Now walk in what I have already won for you."

Paul wrote to the Corinthians: "But thanks be to God, who gives us the victory through our Lord Jesus Christ" (1 Corinthians 15:57).

Notice the tense. He *gives* us the victory. Present tense. Ongoing. Continuous. Not once upon a time. Not someday in the future. Now. Today. In the middle of your battle. In the middle of your valley. In the middle of your struggle.

God never promised us a smooth ride, but He does guarantee a safe landing. The potholes will still come. There will be days when your faith and your love for God feel like they are on the chopping block. There will be nights when you wonder if anyone is listening to your prayers. There will be seasons when the enemy roars so loud you can barely hear the voice of God.

The question in those moments is not, "Am I strong enough?" The question is, "Is Christ enough?"

Resurrection power answers that question with a resounding yes.

RESURRECTION POWER WITHIN THE SOLDIER

The same power that raised Jesus from the dead now lives in you.

This is not religious exaggeration. This is what Scripture actually says.

Paul wrote to the Romans:

But if the Spirit of Him who raised Jesus from the dead dwells in you, He who raised Christ from the dead will also give life to your mortal bodies by His Spirit who dwells in you.

— ROMANS 8:11

Read that again slowly.

The Spirit who raised Jesus from the dead dwells in you. The power that rolled away the stone, that called a dead man back to life, that defeated the grave and launched the greatest comeback in history is the same power that lives inside every believer.

That means you are not just forgiven. You are being transformed. You are not just rescued from hell. You are recruited into a holy army. You are not just surviving life. You are called to advance the Kingdom.

A transformed Kingdom Soldier thinks differently. Prays differently. Responds differently. Fights differently.

Goliath is still big, but God is bigger. The valley is still real, but victory has already been decided at the Cross. The enemy still roars, but his weapons have been disarmed. The battle is still fierce, but the outcome is not in question.

When resurrection power gets hold of a believer's heart, something shifts. Fear loses its grip. Despair loses its voice. Shame loses its authority. You begin to see yourself the way God sees you: not as a victim waiting to be rescued, but as a soldier commissioned to advance.

This is what it means to live from victory, not for it.

THE HOLY SPIRIT: POWER AND COMMUNICATION

Every squad in World War II had someone vital to the mission: the radio operator. His job was not to charge the front line with a rifle. His job was to keep the unit connected to headquarters. Through that one line came orders, air support, intelligence, and rescue.

If the radio went silent, the unit was in trouble. They could still fight. They could still move. But they were cut off from the Commander. They had no idea what was happening in the larger battle. They had no way to call for help.

The Holy Spirit is our divine radio operator. He keeps us connected to Heaven.

He transmits the Commander's voice so we can hear what God is saying. He alerts us to danger before we walk into traps. He gives us the strategy for each battle so we know when to advance and when to hold. He empowers us when our strength is gone so we can keep fighting, even when we feel like quitting.

He is also our power supply.

During World War II, the USS Indianapolis sank in what is

known as the worst open-sea disaster in U.S. Naval History. Communication failure played a vital role in the tragic loss of life. After the ship was sunk by a Japanese submarine, the distress signal was reportedly mishandled, ignored, or never received by several potential listening stations, leading to a significant delay in rescue efforts.[*]

A modern soldier may have the best equipment in the world. Night vision goggles. GPS. Satellite communications. Thermal imaging. But if his batteries are dead, he is armed but powerless. All that technology becomes useless weight.

FRIENDLY FIRE IN AFGHANISTAN (2014)

A "friendly fire" incident that killed five U.S. soldiers and one Afghan was blamed on avoidable miscommunication between U.S. air and ground forces. The air crew and ground forces collectively failed to use proper communication fundamentals and targeting identification procedures, resulting in the mistaken bombing of allied troops.[†]

These two scenarios shows the importance of communication and how vital it is in saving lives.

Many believers are in that condition spiritually. They know Scripture. They know songs. They know church. They have all the right equipment. But they are trying to fight spiritual battles without spiritual power. They are running on empty and wondering why they keep losing ground.

The prophet Zechariah recorded these words from the

---

[*] Phillip Di Tullio, "No Room for Error: How a Breakdown in Naval Communication Led to a Needless Tragedy." *Historical Perspectives: Santa Clara University Undergraduate Journal of History*, 2011, Series II: Vol. 16 , Article 11.

[†] Robert Burns, "Miscommunication Blamed for Deadly U.S. Mistake in Afghanistan." *PBS News*, 5 September 2014, https://www.pbs.org/newshour/nation/miscommunication-blamed-deadly-u-s-mistake-afghanistan.

Lord: "Not by might, nor by power, but by my Spirit, says the LORD of hosts" (Zechariah 4:6).

The Holy Spirit is not a luxury. He is not an accessory. He is not an optional upgrade for advanced believers. He is the life of Christ in you, the presence of God with you, and the power of God working through you.

He also trains you.

Like a drill instructor who pushes recruits to become soldiers, the Spirit pushes, corrects, and disciplines us so we can stand in real battles. He does not coddle us. He does not tell us we are doing fine when we are not. He tells us the truth, even when the truth is uncomfortable, because He loves us too much to leave us unprepared.

Paul wrote to the Romans: "For as many as are led by the Spirit of God, they are the sons of God" (Romans 8:14).

And the psalmist wrote: "He trains my hands to war, and my fingers to fight" (Psalm 144:1).

When you resist His training, you will be unprepared when the battle comes. You will be caught off guard. You will be overwhelmed by things that should not overwhelm you.

But when you submit to His training, you become spiritually fit. Your reflexes sharpen. Your discernment grows. Your faith deepens. You learn to run toward your giants instead of hiding from them.

WORSHIP: THE SOLDIER'S WAR CRY

For a Kingdom Soldier, worship is not just slow songs on Sunday. Worship is surrender. Worship is alignment. Worship is a weapon.

Paul wrote to the Romans, "Present your bodies a living sacrifice, holy, acceptable unto God, which is your reasonable service" (Romans 12:1).

Worship says, "Lord, my life is Yours. My will, my plans, my desires, my strength. Command me."

The English word "worship" comes from the old word *worth-ship*, meaning to give worth or to declare value. When we worship, we are declaring something about God. We are saying, "You are worthy. You are greater than my circumstances. You are more real than my problems. You deserve more than my leftovers."

Worship is a lifestyle, not just a moment. It is obedience, not just emotion. It is a daily posture of bowing our hearts and laying down our swords at the feet of our King.

But worship is also a weapon of warfare.

In 2 Chronicles 20, King Jehoshaphat faced an overwhelming enemy army. God told him the battle was not his but the Lord's. So Jehoshaphat did something that made no military sense. He sent worshipers out in front of the army, singing praises to God. And as they worshiped, the Lord set ambushes against the enemy, and the enemy armies destroyed each other.

In Acts 16, Paul and Silas were beaten, chained, and thrown into the innermost part of a prison. At midnight, instead of complaining or despairing, they worshiped. They sang hymns to God. And as they worshiped, an earthquake shook the prison, the doors flew open, and the chains fell off every prisoner.

When you choose to worship in the middle of a battle, you are not pretending the battle is not real. You are declaring that your God is greater and that the outcome has already been decided at the Cross.

Worship also renews the soldier's strength.

Isaiah wrote:

They that wait upon the LORD shall renew their strength; they shall mount up with wings as eagles; they shall run and not be weary; and they shall walk and not faint.

— ISAIAH 40:31

You cannot worship and stay focused on your giant at the same time. One of them will shrink. Either your God becomes bigger in your eyes or your problem does.

Kingdom Soldiers learn to worship before they see the breakthrough. They learn to praise before the chains fall off. They learn to lift their voices before the walls come down. Because worship is not a response to victory. Worship is part of how victory comes.

SIGNS OF A TRANSFORMED KINGDOM SOLDIER

How do you know resurrection power is at work in a believer's life? What does a transformed Kingdom Soldier look like?

Here are some clear signs.

First, they live from acceptance, not for approval. They know they are loved by God because of Christ, not because of their performance. They serve from gratitude, not for validation. They do not spend their lives trying to earn what has already been given to them freely.

Second, they face battles with confidence in God, not in themselves. Giants still show up. Problems still arise. But their first reflex is to look to the Lord of hosts, not to their own strength. They have learned that their ability is not the issue. God's faithfulness is the issue.

Third, they listen for the Holy Spirit's voice. They do not rush ahead. They do not make decisions based purely on logic or emotion. They are learning to check in with Headquarters before they move. They have cultivated a relationship with the Spirit that allows them to hear His guidance.

Fourth, they use worship as a weapon, not just a warmup.

When storms come, they lift their eyes and their voices. They know the presence of God changes the atmosphere of the battle. They have experienced the power of praise in dark places.

Fifth, they engage the mission. They are not content to sit in the trenches while others fight. They share the Gospel of Grace, make disciples, and step into the assignments God gives them. They understand that they were saved for a purpose and that purpose includes advancing the Kingdom.

Sixth, they get back up. They still stumble. They still have potholes. They still make mistakes. But they do not stay down. They repent, they receive grace, and they get back on the battlefield. They have learned that falling is not failing. Staying down is failing.

LIVING FROM VICTORY

Resurrection power does not remove hardship. It transforms how you walk through it.

You no longer measure your life by the size of your giants, but by the size of your God. You no longer see yourself as a victim of circumstances, but as a soldier under orders. You no longer fight to prove yourself. You fight because Christ has already claimed you.

The battle is real, but the victory is settled. The Cross and the empty tomb are your guarantee.

You are not fighting alone. You are not fighting unarmed. You are not fighting for a crown that might slip away. You are fighting from the finished work of Jesus Christ.

This changes everything.

It changes how you pray. It changes how you face temptation. It changes how you respond to attack. It changes how you handle disappointment. It changes how you view the future.

Because when you know the outcome, you can endure the process.

When you know that Christ has already won, you can face whatever today brings. When you know that your name is written in the Lamb's Book of Life, you do not have to live in fear of what man can do to you. When you know that the same power that raised Jesus from the dead lives in you, you can run toward your Goliath instead of running away.

This is resurrection power.

This is the life of a Kingdom Soldier.

KINGDOM SOLDIER EXERCISE: WRITE YOUR CREED

Every army has a creed, a declaration of who they are and what they stand for. As a Kingdom Soldier, I want to challenge you to write your own.

Use this as a starting point and then make it your own:

My Kingdom Soldier Creed

I am a soldier of the Kingdom of God.
    I have been enlisted by the blood of Jesus Christ.
    I do not fight for victory. I fight from victory,
    because my King has already beaten sin, hell, and the grave.
    I will not live in the trenches of fear and shame.
    I will run toward the battles God calls me to,
    trusting the power of the Holy Spirit within me.
    I will listen for my Commander's voice.
    I will use worship as my weapon, prayer as my lifeline,
    and the Word of God as my sword.
    I will stand for my family, my church, and my generation.
    I will endure hardship as a good soldier of Jesus Christ
    until my King returns or calls me home.

. . .

Now take time to write your own creed in your own words. Put your name on it. Print it. Pray it. Keep it where you can see it.

You are not just a church member. You are a Kingdom Soldier, living in resurrection power, walking in a victory that has already been won.

13

FIELD MANUAL

THE DAILY OPERATIONS
OF A KINGDOM SOLDIER

Up to this point, we have talked about identity, authority, armor, weapons, and battle. We have named the enemy, defined the mission, and clarified what it means to live as a Kingdom Soldier. That foundation matters.

But knowing these things and living them are not the same.

Every army has a field manual. Not a book a soldier reads once and shelves, but a guide he lives by. It governs daily routines, readiness, posture, and response. It exists because battles are rarely won in dramatic moments alone. They are won in preparation. In habits. In discipline practiced long before pressure arrives.

This chapter is not introducing new ideas. It is showing you how a Kingdom Soldier actually lives.

I learned this the hard way. The battles I lost were not because God was absent or unfaithful. They were because I walked onto the field unprepared. I had passion but no rhythm, fire but no formation, calling without consistency. I knew the language of warfare, but I had not yet learned the discipline of daily readiness.

So think of this chapter as a daily briefing. A way of life. A manual for those who refuse to fight casually.

This is not about perfection. It is about posture.

Not about intensity. About consistency.

Not about heroic moments. About faithful ones.

THE BATTLE IN THE DARK

There was a young soldier caught in a nighttime battle that came without warning. One moment, everything was quiet. The next moment, explosions lit up the sky, and the ground shook beneath him. Darkness hid everything except the flashes of fire.

Fear hit him so fast he could barely breathe. He could not see his hand in front of his face. For a moment, he wondered if running for cover would be the wisest thing to do. Every instinct screamed at him to move, to flee, to find somewhere safe. Darkness has a way of making fear feel louder than truth.

Right when panic reached its peak, his radio crackled to life.

It was the voice of his Commander. Firm. Steady. Not panicked. Not uncertain. Calm, clear, and authoritative.

"Hold your position. Reinforcements are on the way."

He told me later he did not feel brave in that moment. His hands were shaking. His heart was pounding. But he trusted that voice. He had heard it before. He had followed it before. Experience had taught him that when the Commander spoke, obedience was the only wise response.

So he calmed his breathing, gripped his weapon, and refused to move. He held his position through the longest night of his life. When dawn broke, the enemy was gone and he was still alive. He did not survive because he was fearless. He survived because he listened.

We all face seasons when the battle comes in the dark. You

cannot see your way forward. You cannot see progress. You cannot see the end. Everything around you feels uncertain, chaotic, and overwhelming.

But you can still hear the voice of the Commander if you have trained your ears to recognize it.

Jesus said, "My sheep hear my voice, and I know them, and they follow me" (John 10:27). Hearing His voice is not a random gift that falls on a few believers and skips the rest. It grows out of relationship. The closer I walk with Him, the clearer His voice becomes. The more time I spend in His presence, the more familiar His tone, His cadence, and His way of speaking become to me.

This is why a Kingdom Soldier lives by a field manual. Daily discipline keeps us in position to hear Him. Daily rhythm keeps us connected to the source of everything we need.

MORNING: REPORTING FOR DUTY

A soldier does not begin the day casually. He begins it consciously.

When I wake up, before I touch my phone or absorb the noise of the world, I report for duty.

"Lord, I'm here. Lead me today."

That simple act sets posture. It reminds me I am not self-directed. I am not reacting to circumstances. I am under command.

Most people wake up and immediately check their phones. They scroll through news, notifications, messages. Before their feet hit the floor, the world has already started shaping their thoughts. They absorb anxiety before they absorb truth. They react before they align.

This is not how soldiers begin.

Prayer is not poetry. It is alignment. It is how I step into the day aware instead of distracted.

I do not ask God to bless my plans. I ask Him to order my steps. One approach treats God like a consultant. The other treats Him like a King.

David understood this: "In the morning, Lord, you hear my voice; in the morning I lay my requests before you and wait expectantly" (Psalm 5:3 NIV). Some mornings, my report is long. Some mornings, it is brief. The length matters less than the posture. What matters is that before the world speaks, God speaks first.

DAILY BREAD: FEEDING BEFORE FIGHTING

No soldier fights well on an empty stomach.

Scripture is not inspiration. It is fuel.

Each day, I take in the Word before the world starts talking. I let truth shape my thinking before lies arrive. I anchor myself in what God has already said so I am not negotiating reality later.

This is not about religious duty. It is about strategic preparation. The enemy does not wait for you to feel ready. He attacks when you are distracted, discouraged, or depleted. If you have not fed on truth, you will have nothing to fight with when pressure comes. You will be left relying on emotion, willpower, or memory. And all three will fail you eventually.

Jesus said, "Man shall not live by bread alone, but by every word that comes from the mouth of God" (Matthew 4:4). He said this while under direct assault from the enemy, and what did He use to fight? Scripture.

Joshua received this command before entering battle: "Keep this Book of the Law always on your lips; meditate on it day and night, so that you may be careful to do everything written in it." Notice the connection. Meditation leads to obedience. Obedience leads to success. Not worldly success, but Kingdom success. Victory in the battles that matter.

Some days, I read a chapter. Some days, I read three verses. Some days, I sit with one sentence until it breaks something open in me. The goal is not volume. The goal is nourishment.

Feed before you fight. Every single day.

GUARDING THE INNER WORLD

Most battles are won or lost internally before anything happens outwardly.

So I guard my mind and heart deliberately.

I do not let emotion define reality. I do not let old shame re-enter my thoughts. I do not rehearse accusations God has already silenced.

This is where many believers lose ground. Not in public, but in private. The battlefield of the mind is where the enemy does his most effective work, and many leave that territory completely undefended.

Think about what happens in your head when you are alone. What do you replay? What do you rehearse? What voices do you listen to when no one else is around?

Paul wrote, "We take captive every thought to make it obedient to Christ" (2 Corinthians 10:5 NIV). That is not passive language. That is warfare language.

When shame says, "You will never change," truth says, "If anyone is in Christ, he is a new creation."

When fear says, "You are alone," truth says, "I will never leave you nor forsake you."

When accusation says, "God is done with you," truth says, "There is now no condemnation for those who are in Christ Jesus."

Feelings are real. They are not reliable. A guarded inner life leaves the enemy very little room to operate.

Guard yours.

WALKING STEADY: PEACE AS FOOTING

Peace is not passivity. It is footing.

The soldier who panics is the soldier who falls. Anxiety clouds judgment, accelerates bad decisions, and opens doors the enemy is waiting to walk through.

Paul described feet fitted with the readiness of the Gospel of peace. Not just peace as a feeling, but peace as equipment. Peace as stability.

Peace keeps me from reacting in the flesh when pressure shows up. It keeps me from rushing. It keeps me from striving to control outcomes. It keeps my steps deliberate.

There is a difference between urgency and panic. Urgency responds to what matters. Panic reacts to everything. Urgency is focused. Panic is scattered.

When peace lifts, I pause. When peace remains, I move.

This becomes a guidance system. The Holy Spirit often leads through peace. He can restrain with a check in your spirit. He can confirm with steady calm, even when the situation is hard.

A steady soldier is far more effective than a frantic one.

FAITH IN REAL TIME

Faith is not a surge of confidence. It is a settled decision.

Most people think of faith as something they summon in a crisis. They strain for belief when trouble hits.

That is not how soldiers live.

Faith is not reactive. It is preemptive.

Before the day unfolds, I settle this: God is faithful. God is present. God is at work. When fear, doubt, or discouragement shows up, it meets a shield that is already raised.

The shield of faith is not grabbed in the moment of attack. It is carried into battle already lifted. When the arrow flies, it is too late to start looking for your shield.

Hebrews calls faith "confidence" and "assurance." Faith does not wait to see how things turn out. It trusts the One who holds the outcome.

Doubt says, "What if it does not work out?" Faith says, "God is working."

Fear says, "You cannot handle this." Faith says, "Christ strengthens me."

Accusation says, "You have failed too many times." Faith says, "His mercies are new every morning."

Raise your shield before the battle begins. Keep it up all day.

THE WORD SPOKEN, NOT STORED

Scripture is not decorative.

Many read the Bible. Fewer speak it. And there is a difference.

When pressure comes, I speak the Word. Out loud, if necessary. I answer lies with truth. I confront temptation with Scripture. I refuse to let thoughts spiral unchallenged.

Jesus fought this way. In the wilderness, every time the enemy attacked, Jesus responded with, "It is written." Not "I feel." Not "I think." Not "I hope." The Word.

There is power in spoken truth. The lie that was whispering in your head meets truth spoken from your lips.

The Word in my mouth becomes strength in my life.

This requires storing Scripture ahead of time. You are not just collecting information. You are loading ammunition.

A sword in the sheath does no good. Draw it. Use it. Speak it.

STAYING CONNECTED TO COMMAND

No soldier fights independently.

In human armies, soldiers who lose communication with command become vulnerable. They do not know what is happening elsewhere on the battlefield. They cannot receive updated orders. They make decisions based on incomplete information.

The same is true spiritually.

Prayer keeps me connected to God's strategy. It keeps me from fighting battles I was never assigned. It keeps me sensitive to correction and direction.

Some days prayer feels like fire. Some days it feels like discipline. Both are necessary.

Prayer is not only me talking. It is me listening. Receiving direction. Correction. Strength.

"Lord, what is mine to do today?"

That question keeps me focused. It prevents overextension. It keeps me within my assignment.

DAILY INSPECTION: CHECK YOUR SEALS

Richard the plumber in me understands this. A pipe is only as strong as its seal. A small leak might not seem like a big deal at first. Just a drip. But if that leak is not fixed, it becomes a larger problem. Damage spreads. What started small becomes costly.

A small compromise becomes a collapse if it is not addressed. A small drift becomes a detour. A small neglect becomes a habit. Before you know it, you have wandered far from where you were supposed to be.

So inspect your connections. Check your prayer life. Is there a leak? Check your integrity. Is there a crack? Check your obedience. Is there a drip? Check your relationships. Is there damage? Check your thought life. Is there contamination?

This is not condemnation. This is maintenance.

AWARENESS WITHOUT FEAR

Kingdom Soldiers stay alert, not anxious.

Alertness is awareness. It is paying attention. It is recognizing we are in a battle and acting accordingly. Alertness keeps you ready.

Anxiety is fear dressed up as vigilance. It is exhausting yourself watching for threats that may never come. Anxiety keeps you paralyzed.

Peter wrote, "Be sober, be vigilant; because your adversary the devil, as a roaring lion, walketh about" (1 Peter 5:8 KJV). He did not say be terrified. He said be alert.

I pay attention to atmospheres, conversations, unrest, and opportunity. The Holy Spirit leads quietly, but clearly, when we are listening.

The soldier who ignores his environment gets ambushed. The soldier who obsesses over threats gets exhausted. The soldier who stays alert stays effective.

BROTHERHOOD AND SUPPORT

Isolation weakens soldiers.

The enemy knows this. One of his primary tactics is to convince you that you are alone. That no one else struggles the way you do. That your battles are too shameful to share. That you are better off fighting solo.

That is a lie.

I stay connected to other believers. I give encouragement and receive it. I allow others to speak into my life. Unity strengthens resolve. Accountability keeps me grounded.

Ecclesiastes says, "A cord of three strands is not quickly

broken" (Ecclesiastes 4:12 NIV). Moses needed Aaron and Hur to hold up his arms during battle. Without them, he would have failed. With them, Israel won.

You need people who will fight with you. People who will tell you the truth. People who will lift your arms when you are tired.

Do not isolate. Do not pretend. Do not fight alone.

HOLDING YOUR POST

Every soldier has an assignment.

Not every soldier storms the front line. Not every soldier leads a charge. Some guard supply lines. Some hold territory. Some serve in ways that never make headlines but are essential to victory.

Each day I ask, "Lord, what is my assignment today?"

This question keeps me from two dangers.

The first danger is passivity: assuming I have no role, no post, no responsibility. That is not humility. That is abdication.

The second danger is overreach: assuming I am responsible for everything. That leads to exhaustion and defeat. Not every battle is yours. Not every hill is worth dying on.

The enemy will try to distract you, discourage you, or pull you away from your post. God strengthens you to stand faithfully in your place.

THE SOLDIER WHO WOULD NOT LEAVE HIS POST

There was a soldier in World War II assigned to guard a small bridge. Nothing glamorous. Not the front line. Not the kind of assignment they write movies about. Just a bridge in the middle of nowhere.

But that bridge was the only route the enemy could use to reach the base. If that soldier left his post, the entire camp would be vulnerable. Everything depended on him staying where he was assigned.

One night, a terrible storm blew in. Rain hit him like needles. Wind cut through his uniform. Thunder shook the ground. Hours passed with no relief. No shelter. No backup. Just him, the storm, and the bridge.

He could have walked away. No one would have known. The officers were far away. The other soldiers were asleep. He could have left and returned before anyone noticed.

But he stayed.

When the officer finally arrived the next morning, he looked at the soldier standing soaked and exhausted at his post and said, "Son, why did you stand here all night? You could have left. No one would have known."

The soldier answered simply, "Sir, I did not stay because someone saw me. I stayed because I gave my word. If I leave my post, the enemy advances. This is my assignment."

That story has stayed with me for years.

Your post might be your home. Your marriage. Your prayer life. Your children. Your integrity at work. Your calling. A ministry no one applauds. A burden God placed in your spirit that no one else sees or understands.

But it is your post.

Nehemiah said it the way every Kingdom Soldier needs to learn to say it: "I am doing a great work, so that I cannot come down" (Nehemiah 6:3 KJV).

Stay faithful. Staying at your post is not small. It is warfare.

WHEN YOU GET HIT

Every soldier takes hits.

If you fight, you will get hit. If you advance against the

enemy, he will strike back. If you live faithfully in a fallen world, you will face setbacks, failures, and falls.

The question is not whether you will get hit. The question is what you will do when you do.

When I fall, I respond quickly. I confess. I receive grace. I reject shame. I re-engage obedience without retreating into self-condemnation.

Many men fall and then stay down. Shame keeps them on the ground. They believe the lie, "You failed, so you are a failure." They withdraw from God instead of running to Him.

That is exactly what the enemy wants.

Proverbs says, "Though the righteous fall seven times, they rise again" (Proverbs 24:16 NIV). The righteous fall. Not the wicked. Falling is not the opposite of righteousness. Staying down is.

If we confess our sins, He is faithful and just to forgive and cleanse.

So confess quickly. Receive grace fully. Reject shame completely. Restore fellowship immediately. Step back into obedience without delay.

A fallen soldier who gets up is still dangerous.

WALKING WITH THE SPIRIT

The Holy Spirit leads the march.

You are not operating on your own wisdom, your own strength, or your own strategy. The Spirit of God lives within you and guides you.

I follow His nudges. I respect His restraint. I move when peace remains. I pause when it lifts.

His guidance is usually quiet. A check in your spirit. A thought that will not leave. An open door. A closed one.

My responsibility is obedience. His responsibility is outcome.

"Since we live by the Spirit, let us keep in step with the Spirit."

Keep in step. Not running ahead. Not lagging behind. Walking in sync with the One who leads.

LIVING DEPLOYED

My gifts are not trophies. They are tools.

Every Kingdom Soldier has been equipped with something. Gifts. Abilities. Resources. Relationships. These are not given for accumulation or admiration. They are given for deployment.

Each day, I look for opportunities to use what God has placed in my hands. Encouragement. Prayer. Truth spoken with humility. A practical act of service. A quiet moment of courage. A faithful word at the right time.

Do not wait for the big moment. Use what you have today.

The parable of the talents makes it clear. The master did not reward the servant who protected what he was given. He rewarded the servants who used it.

You are not in storage. You are on assignment.

Live deployed.

THE KINGDOM SOLDIER LIFESTYLE

Being a Kingdom Soldier is not something you turn on in crisis. It is a way of life.

Daily surrender. Daily obedience. Daily readiness.

This is how soldiers are formed. This is how battles are won. This is how faith endures.

And once you learn to live this way, you do not keep it to yourself.

You train another.

The Kingdom was never meant to be carried by a few. It was

always meant to be carried by an army. The soldier who learns to fight trains another who learns to fight who trains another who learns to fight.

Sound the alarm.

Watch God multiply what He has given you.

Your soldier is waiting.

14

SOUND THE ALARM

RAISING THE NEXT SOLDIERS

There comes a time in every soldier's life when they realize the mission cannot stop with them. I have fought many battles and walked through many trials. I have poured my life into the calling God placed on me.

But none of that will matter if I fail at the one thing every Kingdom Soldier must eventually do: train the next one.

Moses had Joshua.

Elijah had Elisha.

Paul had Timothy.

But Joshua never trained a successor, and the nation felt the impact of that gap. Judges tells us that after Joshua and his generation died, there arose a generation who did not know the Lord or the works He had done. The chain broke. The baton dropped.

The vision God puts in your heart can keep living after you are gone if you prepare others to carry it.

A soldier who fights alone may win a battle.

A soldier who trains others can win a generation.

The Apostle Paul understood this deeply. He did not just preach sermons and move on. He planted his life like a seed in people. He knew the Great Commission from our Commander in Chief, Jesus Christ, was to make disciples, not just converts. He knew that the Kingdom would advance as disciples became disciple makers.

Paul wrote to his spiritual son Timothy:

And the things that thou hast heard of me among many witnesses, the same commit thou to faithful men, who shall be able to teach others also.

— 2 TIMOTHY 2:2 KJV

In that one verse, you can see four spiritual generations:

Christ poured into Paul.

Paul poured into Timothy.

Timothy poured into faithful men.

Those faithful men taught others also.

This is Heaven's multiplication plan. Not one hero doing all the work, but an army of trained soldiers who carry the mission forward.

The Gospel did not spread across the world only through crowds and crusades. It spread through training. Through kitchens and marketplaces, prison cells and living rooms. Through believers who understood that what God gave them was never meant to stop with them.

This is not accidental. It is intentional. It is the way God designed His Kingdom to grow.

The Law of Multiplication works like this:

1. Believers are trained.
2. Those believers train others.
3. Those others train still more.
4. Over time, impact multiplies far beyond the original investment.

You can see this law written into creation itself. One seed becomes a tree. That tree produces many seeds. Those seeds become more trees. Given time, a single seed can fill a forest. No seed panics because it cannot become a forest overnight. It simply grows, produces, and trusts the process God designed.

Spiritually, it works the same way.

If one believer follows Jesus faithfully and pours into just one person a year, and that person learns to do the same, multiplication begins quietly. It does not look impressive at first. It never does. But ten years later, you do not have a small group clinging to one leader. You have a movement. You have generations of believers who know how to walk with God, stand in battle, and train others to do the same.

This is why discipleship is not about crowds. It is about depth. Jesus did not start with thousands. He started with twelve. And even among the twelve, He invested deeply in a few. He was not rushed. He was intentional.

One of the primary goals of a disciple maker is not to create dependence. It is to create maturity. You are not raising spiritual infants who will always need to be spoon-fed. You are raising soldiers who know how to suit up, listen to the Commander, and stand their post when you are not around.

A disciple who can only survive when you are present has not been fully trained. A disciple who can feed himself, discern God's voice, resist the enemy, and obey under pressure is someone who is ready to train others.

This is not random. It is deliberate.

Discipleship is not just a class you attend or a book you finish. It is not information transfer alone. It is life-on-life formation. It is walking with someone through Scripture, prayer, obedience, failure, repentance, and growth. It is letting them see how you respond when you are under pressure, how you recover when you stumble, how you listen for God's direction, and how you keep going when the battle is hard.

It requires presence.

It requires patience.

It requires consistency.

You will not always see immediate results. Some seeds take time to break the soil. Some roots grow deep before anything shows on the surface. Discipleship often feels slow, quiet, and unseen. That does not mean it is ineffective. It means it is working the way God designed it to work.

This is a marathon, not a sprint.

But the fruit is lasting. Long after programs fade and personalities are forgotten, disciples who make disciples remain. They carry the mission forward. They protect the Kingdom from becoming shallow. They ensure that the faith does not stop with one generation.

This is how the Kingdom advances.

This is how soldiers reproduce.

This is how the mission continues long after we are gone.

And this is why no Kingdom Soldier is ever finished when he finishes his own training. The mission is not complete until what God has built in you begins to multiply through others.

A PARENT HEART: SONS AND DAUGHTERS OF THE KINGDOM

When Paul wrote to the Thessalonian church, he used the language of family to describe how he had ministered to them. He said he was like a gentle nursing mother and like an encouraging father. That is a parent heart.

A parent heart says, "I am not just here to preach to you. I am here to care for you, to walk with you, to help you grow."

As a parent of four, I have watched my children grow through many stages. Each season brought new challenges and new joys. As babies, they needed everything. Food. Protection.

Comfort. Clean clothes. As they grew, they learned to feed themselves, walk, run, and take responsibility.

If I had expected my toddlers to act like adults, I would have crushed them. If I had expected my teenagers to stay like toddlers, I would have held them back. Parenting means meeting a child where they are and walking them toward maturity.

New believers are just the same.

At first, they need more support. They make messes. They ask basic questions. They fall down and cry. A spiritual parent does not shame them for that. A spiritual parent knows this is part of growth.

A spiritual parent teaches a new believer how to feed themselves by:

Helping them learn how to pray.

Showing them how to study the Word of God.

Teaching them the importance of fellowship and belonging to a church family.

Encouraging them to take notes, to listen, to learn.

Modeling how to share their faith with others.

Showing them how obedience grows strong roots.

Today, the Body of Christ is experiencing what I call the revolving door syndrome. People come in, respond to an altar call, feel a touch of God, and then slip away, because no one embraced them with a parent heart.

They did not need a lecture. They needed a parent.

A parent loves, feeds, protects, encourages, and cleans the baby when they make a mess. A new believer needs someone who will keep caring when they stumble, when they fall, and when old habits surface again.

Over the years, many younger believers have called me Pops or Dad. They were not honoring my perfection. They were simply responding to presence.

One of them was a young man named Lawrence. He was

about twenty years old and had been saved for around a year. I assumed at first that our shared love for running and weightlifting was what drew him close. One day, he corrected me and said it was my passion for teaching the Word of God and my compassion for people.

Lawrence came from a broken home. His parents' divorce left wounds in his heart that did not heal overnight. I had the privilege of walking with him through that season. We talked, prayed, studied, and trained together.

Later he transferred out of state to Arizona to complete his senior year of college. Even from a distance, he would remind me of the impact those years had on his life. I believe he has continued to pour into others what God poured into him.

That is the fruit of a parent heart.

A SERVANT HEART: PAYING THE COST OF DISCIPLESHIP

Jesus told His disciples, "Whoever would be great among you must be your servant" (Matthew 20:26). In the Kingdom, greatness is not measured by how many people serve you, but by how many people you serve.

If we are going to make disciples, we must have a servant heart.

A servant heart is not a title or position. It is an attitude. It shows up in small, often unnoticed ways. It may mean:

Answering a phone call late at night.

Rearranging your schedule to meet for coffee.

Giving a ride, sharing a meal, or opening your home.

Investing finances so someone can attend a retreat, a conference, or a class.

A servant heart says, "I am willing to be inconvenienced for the sake of someone else's growth."

A servant heart is attractive. People sense it. It disarms their defenses. It helps them feel safe enough to be honest. It reflects the heart of Jesus, who came not to be served, but to serve and to give His life as a ransom for many.

Nothing changes lives like relationships.

But many of us have buckets filled with good things that crowd out the Great Commission. We have filled our schedules with meetings, entertainment, and religious activity. We stay busy with church work and forget the work of the Church, which is to make disciples.

We forget that people are perishing without Christ. We forget the eternal state of friends, coworkers, neighbors, and family members who do not know Him. Our hearts grow numb.

Meanwhile, Jesus is still saying, "Go and make disciples."

So many in the Body of Christ are content with being church members. Membership with no commitment is a sign that someone has not been discipled yet.

Disciples make disciples. It is in their spiritual DNA. Jesus poured His life into His disciples and expected them to pour their lives into others. He still expects it today.

My friend, we have loved ones imprisoned by sin and longing to be free. Some of them have wounded you. Some have disappointed you so many times that you stopped expecting change.

But you cannot give up. Not when the Lord refused to give up on you.

BROTHERS IN ARMS: THE SOLDIER'S CIRCLE

The phrase "brothers in arms" has been used for centuries to describe the bond between soldiers who have faced danger together. They have stood shoulder to shoulder under fire.

They have buried friends together. They have shared victories and losses.

In that kind of environment, the relationship goes deeper than friendship. It becomes brotherhood.

In the Body of Christ, we are meant to experience this same kind of camaraderie.

No soldier survives without a unit. That is true in war, and it is true in the Kingdom. The loner Christian who tries to follow Jesus by himself is an easy target. The soldier who separates from the platoon is exposed.

Every significant breakthrough I have seen in my life has been connected to brothers and sisters standing with me. Praying with me. Correcting me. Encouraging me. Fighting beside me.

A Kingdom Soldier needs:

Someone who sharpens him.

Someone who prays with him.

Someone who holds him up when he is weary.

Someone he can pour into.

Someone who will continue the mission after he is gone.

During my eleven years as a senior pastor, I taught often from Paul's picture of the body in Corinthians. Just as the human body has many parts, each with a different function, the Church needs every member operating in their spiritual gift for the whole to stay healthy.

My goal was to help each person recognize their God-given gift, develop and use that gift, and then honor the gifts in others.

Over time, I watched people step into their roles. Teachers began to teach. Encouragers began to encourage. Intercessors began to pray with focus. Leaders began to lead teams. Mercy givers began to show compassion in powerful ways. The church began to move like a healthy body instead of a handful of parts.

Healthy churches advance the Kingdom.

The devil hates this kind of unity. He has used denomination, race, politics, preferences, and finances to divide the Body of Christ.

But regardless of denomination, we are one Body. We serve the same Commander in Chief, Jesus Christ.

When we recognize that we need each other to complete the Great Commission, we will see a supernatural harvest of lives transformed.

ONE BAND, ONE SOUL: THE POWER OF UNITY

In the movie *Drumline*, the band director drills his students with a simple phrase: one band, one sound. His point is that unity matters more than individual talent.[*]

A gifted drummer who refuses to follow the rhythm weakens the entire band. No matter how skilled he is, if he plays his own beat, the performance falls apart.

For the Army of God, the phrase could be: one Kingdom, one Commander, one sound.

Jesus prayed that we would be one. Paul urged the churches to be of the same mind and spirit. The early church in Acts saw power, miracles, and rapid growth because they walked in one accord.

Unity is not about everyone looking the same, sounding the same, or having the same personality. Unity is shared allegiance. It is a common purpose. It is marching to the same drum, the heartbeat of our King.

Division weakens.

Isolation destroys.

Unity multiplies strength.

When we train others, we are not just helping individuals.

---

[*] *Drumline*. Directed by Charles Stone III. Fox 2000 Pictures, 2002.

We are strengthening the whole army. Every soldier you raise becomes another shield, another sword, another intercessor, another voice of truth, another torch in the darkness.

If the Body of Christ moved like a single, trained, aligned force under the same Commander, the gates of hell would not just tremble. They would fall.

LEAVING A LEGACY THAT OUTLIVES YOU

Your legacy is not formed in a single moment. It is shaped quietly, day after day, by the choices you make when no one is watching.

It is shaped by your obedience, both in public and in private. The moments when you say yes to God even when obedience costs you comfort, reputation, or ease. Heaven notices the quiet obedience just as much as the visible one, and often more. Faithfulness in unseen places builds strength that shows up later in visible ways.

Your legacy is also formed by your integrity. Integrity is who you are when there is no audience and no pressure to perform. It is choosing truth when compromise would go unnoticed. It is living the same life in private that you present in public. A soldier with integrity can be trusted with influence, because his foundation is solid.

Your willingness to sacrifice shapes legacy as well. Time, money, energy, and comfort are the currencies of discipleship. Kingdom impact always costs something. When you choose to invest yourself in others instead of protecting your own convenience, you are planting seeds that will grow long after you are gone.

Prayer is another unseen place where legacy is built. Intercession does not draw attention, but it moves Heaven. When you carry people before God in prayer, you are participating in battles you may never see. Some breakthroughs happen years after the prayer is prayed, but Heaven never forgets a faithful intercessor.

Worship also leaves a mark, especially when it rises from the valley. Anyone can worship on the mountaintop. But worship offered in pain, confusion, or loss carries a different weight. It teaches those watching, and those who come after you, that God is worthy even when circumstances are not favorable. That kind of worship becomes a testimony that outlives you.

All of these moments add up. Together, they form a legacy that is not loud but is lasting. A Kingdom Soldier's legacy is not carved into buildings or plaques. It is carved into lives. It is written in the testimonies of people who walk stronger in Christ because you walked with them. It is recorded in Heaven, where faithfulness is never forgotten and obedience always matters.

That is the kind of legacy that endures.

SOUNDING THE ALARM

We are living in a time when many believers are asleep in their calling. Some sit in church week after week and never step onto the battlefield. They love God, but they have never been trained or challenged to join the fight.

Jesus said the harvest is plentiful, but the laborers are few. The problem is not the lack of souls ready to hear. The problem is the lack of soldiers ready to go.

You and I have heard the alarm.

We know the urgency.

We feel the weight.

We understand the times.

Now it is our responsibility to sound the alarm for someone else.

Call them out.

Train them up.

Stand beside them until they can stand on their own.

A soldier has not finished his mission until he has helped secure the next generation.

A SIMPLE TRAINING PATTERN: HOW TO RAISE YOUR FIRST SOLDIER

The enemy loves to whisper that discipling others is too complicated. That you are not smart enough, trained enough, educated enough, holy enough.

The truth is much simpler. If you can love Jesus, open your Bible, and show up, you can train a soldier.

Here is a simple pattern you can follow.

1. Identify One Person

Ask God to show you someone who:

- Respects your walk with God.
- Is spiritually hungry.
- Could grow under your leadership.

This may be a younger believer at church, a coworker who keeps asking you questions, a neighbor who opens up about their struggles, or someone who always seems to light up when you talk about the Lord.

I remember teaching a Bible study one night when a man suddenly stood up in the middle of the lesson and said, "I want to be saved." It surprised me, but I invited him forward and we prayed. He gave his life to Christ that night.

Later he told me what happened. He had seen a flyer posted on the bulletin board in his apartment complex that afternoon. The words that drew him were simple:

"You do not have to remain the same when Jesus can change you."

He said those words spoke directly to his heart. He was tired of his life, tired of drinking, tired of running. He came to the Bible study because he was desperate for change.

We spent years walking together after that. He traveled with me to speaking engagements and conferences. That one response to a flyer turned into a long season of discipleship and friendship.

Your first soldier may come to you in a way that surprises you. Pay attention.

2. Meet with Them Consistently

Weekly or biweekly is usually enough. The key is consistency, not perfection.

Meet for coffee, a meal, a walk, or at church. Keep it simple. Show up. Listen. Share. Pray.

3. Share Scripture and Life Lessons

You do not have to preach a polished sermon. Share a passage of Scripture and talk about how it applies to real life. Share what God has taught you through your own struggles and victories.

Let them ask questions. If you do not know the answer, say so, and then search the Scriptures together. That humility builds trust.

4. Pray Together

Teach them how to talk to God, not just about God. Let them hear you pray honestly.

Encourage them to pray in their own words. Show them

that God listens to real, raw, honest prayers, not just religious phrases.

Prayer creates a bond between you and opens a channel for the Holy Spirit to work deeply.

5. Model Spiritual Habits

Let them see your discipline. Invite them to join you in activities like:

- Reading Scripture.
- Attending church faithfully.
- Serving in practical ways.
- Fasting on occasion.
- Worshiping with intention.

They will learn as much from what you do as from what you say.

6. Give Them Assignments

Start small. Ask them to:

- Read a chapter and share what God showed them.
- Memorize a simple verse.
- Share their testimony with one person.
- Help serve at church one Sunday.

Small steps of obedience build strong soldiers. Every time they step out and God meets them, their faith grows.

7. Send Them to Train Another

Multiplication is the final step of discipleship. You are not finished when they can stand. You are finished when they can train.

Encourage them to begin asking the Lord for their own Timothy. Walk with them as they begin discipling someone else. Stay available to coach them, but let them carry the responsibility.

This is how spiritual family multiplies. This is how the Kingdom spreads.

EXERCISE: RECRUIT YOUR FIRST TRAINEE

Returning to Step 1, take a moment and write down the names of three people who:

- Respect your walk with God.
- Are spiritually hungry.
- Could grow under your leadership.

Now circle one name.

This is your first soldier.

This is your assignment.

This is how the Kingdom grows.

Pray over that name. Ask the Lord:

"Commander, is this the one You are assigning to me in this season?"

If you sense His yes, reach out. Invite them to start meeting regularly to talk about following Jesus together. You may feel nervous. That is normal. Step forward anyway.

The first step is often the hardest. After that, you will begin to see the Holy Spirit do what only He can do.

FINAL CHARGE: SOUND THE ALARM

I have fought many battles in my life. Some were loud and public. Others were fought quietly, in prayer, in obedience, and in endurance when quitting would have been easier. But the most important battles I ever fought were not for my own survival or success. They were fought so that someone else could rise, so that another soldier could find their footing, and so that the mission would continue long after my strength was spent.

That is why I now place the same charge in your hands that Paul placed in Timothy's.

Train faithful men and women. Not perfect ones. Not polished ones. Faithful ones. Those who are willing to learn, willing to obey, and willing to keep going when the road gets hard. Invest your time, your wisdom, and your life in people who will carry the mission forward with integrity.

Strengthen the next soldier. Walk with them. Pray with them. Correct them when needed. Encourage them when they are weary. Help them put on their armor and teach them how to stand. Do not rush them through the process. Soldiers are not formed overnight. They are forged through relationship, repetition, and trust.

Multiply the mission. The Kingdom was never designed to rest on a single leader, a single church, or a single generation. What God has entrusted to you is meant to pass through you, not stop with you. When you train one who trains another, you step into Heaven's strategy for lasting impact.

The Kingdom of God was never meant to be carried by a few. It was always meant to be carried by an army. Ordinary men and women, awakened to their identity, armed with truth, and committed to obedience. When each soldier takes responsibility for another, the enemy loses ground and the Kingdom advances.

So sound the alarm.

Wake up what has been sleeping. Call out the soldier God has placed in your path. Speak life into them. Walk beside them. Refuse to let fear, comfort, or distraction silence the call.

Then step back and watch God do what only He can do.

He will multiply what you have given. He will advance His Kingdom through faithful hands. He will raise up soldiers who will one day raise others.

Your soldier is waiting.

15

THE KINGDOM SOLDIER'S
ULTIMATE CALL

I want to begin by thanking you for walking through this book with me. My aim has been simple. I wanted you to know that you are part of God's plan to advance His Kingdom on the earth. You are not a spectator. You are not an extra piece in the box. You are a key part of His strategy.

Everything you have read to this point—all the stories, all the battles, all the truths and teachings—brings us to this final call.

You were created to worship the King.

You were created to serve Him.

You were created to advance His Kingdom.

Your assignment matters far more than you may realize.

This is not the moment to sit down.

This is the moment to rise.

Let me share with you what is on my heart as we close this journey together.

THE COMING KING AND ETERNAL REWARDS

There is a day coming when every Kingdom Soldier will stand before the King. Jesus will return, not as the Lamb who was slain, but as the King who reigns. And when we stand before Him, He will not ask about titles or reputation. He will ask what we did with what He placed in our hands.

The parable of the talents in Matthew 25 still shakes me. The man who buried his gift did not lose it because he was wicked. He lost it because he underestimated it. He lived small when he had been entrusted with great potential.

I know that feeling. I have felt unqualified. I have questioned whether what I carried mattered. But the King does not measure success by our credentials. He measures faithfulness.

The man who buried his talent never heard the words, "Well done." I refuse to live in a way that robs me of that moment. And I do not want you to miss it, either.

God placed something inside you: gifts, stories, wisdom, compassion, scars that became strength, experiences that became fire. None of it is accidental. None of it is wasted.

One day, you will stand before the King, and everything else in this life will fade. What remains is what you did for Him.

I want you to be ready.

THE HARVEST AND THE NEED FOR SOLDIERS

We live in a world groaning under the weight of brokenness. People are carrying silent battles of trauma, addiction, shame, and fear. Families are fractured. Young people cannot find their footing. Depression and anxiety are robbing men and women of their identity.

This is why the harvest is great.

This is why the Kingdom needs soldiers.

Converts do not advance the Kingdom.

Disciples do.

I stand here today because someone discipled me. Someone walked beside me. Someone prayed with me. Someone believed in the work of God in my life, even before I believed it myself.

That is how transformation happens.

That is how the Kingdom advances.

That is how soldiers are formed.

There are people in your life who will never hear the Gospel unless you speak it. There are battles that will never be won unless you take your place. There are hearts that will never heal unless you step into their story.

The harvest is ready.

The time for silence is over.

The time for hesitation is over.

You are needed now.

MY PERSONAL JOURNEY AND WHY I CANNOT STAY QUIET

When I think back over my early walk with God, I see the faces of the people who refused to give up on me. They prayed for me. They showed up for me. They walked with me through my contradictions and brokenness. They lived the Gospel in front of me.

They wore me down with love.

They wore me down with consistency.

They wore me down by being the same person in private that they were in public.

That is how discipleship works.

That is how chains break.

That is how men and women are transformed.

Everything I have written in this book flows from that experience. Someone discipled me. Someone invested in me. Someone believed in the call of God on my life. Now, I want to do the same for you.

What God did in me, He wants to do through me.

What God did in you, He wants to do through you.

This is why I cannot stay quiet.

This is why this book exists.

This is why you are reading these words.

RISE UP AND STEP OUT

Let me speak to you directly.

If you are reading this, you were drawn here by the Spirit of God. You are not here by coincidence. You are here because God has been stirring something inside you.

It is time to rise up.

It is time to step out.

It is time to stop waiting for perfect conditions.

It is time to stop believing the lie that you have nothing to offer.

I do not care what your background is.

I do not care what mistakes are in your past.

I do not care how unprepared you feel.

If you are a housewife, rise up.

If you are a plumber, rise up.

If you are a teacher, rise up.

If you are a lawyer or doctor, rise up.

If you are an ex-drug addict, rise up.

If you are an ex-inmate, rise up.

If you are young or old, rise up.

If you feel forgotten or unseen, rise up.

If Jesus reached you, He can reach them.

And He wants to reach them through you.

The world does not need more passive believers.

The world needs Kingdom Soldiers who will carry the message of reconciliation wherever they go.

You are the one He is calling.

YOUR KINGDOM SOLDIER COMMISSION

You have walked with me through surrender, warfare, discipline, purpose, identity, endurance, and discipleship. Now, it is time for your commissioning.

This is not my commission.

This is not your church's commission.

This is the commission of the King.

"Go and make disciples."

You are called to worship Him with your whole life.

You are called to bring His presence into your world.

You are called to speak life into broken places.

You are called to fight darkness with the authority He gave you.

You are called to carry the Good News.

By the authority of the Word of God, I commission you today as a Kingdom Soldier in the Army of the Lord.

Stand tall.

Step forward.

Use what He placed in you.

Do not bury your gift.

Do not underestimate your assignment.

From every culture, every occupation, and every corner of the earth, He is assembling His last-day army—men and women who will preach reconciliation, set captives free, and bind up the brokenhearted.

The King has need of you.

Serve Him with passion.

Worship Him with your life.

Fight with courage.
Love people deeply.
Disciple others faithfully.
And keep marching until the King returns.

LOVE YOU,
Richard "Cuzz" Robinson

THE KINGDOM SOLDIER CREED
APPENDIX A

I am a Kingdom Soldier.

I belong to the King of Kings and the Lord of Lords.

I am enlisted in His service, trained by His Spirit, and empowered by His Word.

As a Kingdom Soldier, I advance with purpose, authority, and obedience to God.

I advance by growing spiritually.

I advance by deepening my prayer life.

I advance by living by the Word and walking in the Spirit.

I refuse to remain where I am when God calls me forward.

I do not fear the battlefield, and I do not retreat.

I walk in holiness and courage.

I resist temptation and tear down strongholds.

I grow stronger, wiser, and more effective.

I allow God to transform my character, and I let go of old habits.

I shine the love and light of Christ in dark places.

I embrace my identity in Christ so that I may war effectively.

I stand clothed in the full armor of God.

I wear the belt of Truth so that I may walk in integrity.

I guard my heart with the breastplate of Righteousness.

My steps are guided by the Gospel of Peace.

I lift the shield of Faith to extinguish every attack of the enemy.

My mind is secured by the helmet of Salvation.

I wield the Sword of the Spirit, the living and active Word of God.

I do not fight against flesh and blood.

I wage war in the Spirit with prayer, faith, and obedience.

I walk in love, stand in courage, and endure with patience.

I am not my own.

I serve under the command of the Holy One.

Where He sends, I will go.

What He speaks, I will obey.

When He calls, I will answer.

I will not retreat.

I will not surrender to fear.

I will not abandon my post.

The Greater One lives within me.

I stand with my brothers and sisters in the Kingdom.

I lift the weary.

I encourage the broken.

I defend the weak.

My mission is clear.

By God's authority, in Jesus' name, through the power of the Holy Spirit,

in life, in death, and in eternity,

I belong to the King.

I advance.

A FIELD GUIDE FOR KINGDOM SOLDIERS

This appendix is not new material.

It is a compression of what you have already learned.

Use it when you are under pressure.

Use it when clarity is fading.

Use it when the battle feels confusing.

1. Know the Nature of the War

The battle is spiritual, not personal.

Your enemy is not people, politics, institutions, or personalities.

Ephesians 6:12

The enemy's primary tactics:

- Deception
- Accusation
- Fear
- Distraction

- Isolation
- Condemnation

His goal is not always destruction.
Often it is drift, discouragement, or silencing.
If you are fighting people, you are already misaligned.

2. Know Your Position Before You Fight

You fight from victory, not for it.
    Colossians 2:15
    Your authority flows from identity, not effort.
    You stand in Christ, not in performance.
    Standing means:

- No retreat in faith
- No surrender of ground
- No negotiating truth

If you forget who you are, every weapon feels heavy.

3. The Armor of God: Operational Summary

This is not metaphor. This is daily equipment.

Belt of Truth

- Truth holds everything together.
- Measure thoughts, emotions, and assumptions against Scripture.
- Confusion creates vulnerability.

Breastplate of Righteousness

- Rest in Christ's righteousness.
- Live righteously in obedience.
- Compromise exposes the heart.

Shoes of Peace

- Peace is footing, not passivity.
- Panic weakens judgment.
- Move deliberately, not reactively.

Shield of Faith

- Faith is settled trust, not emotional surge.
- Raise it before the attack comes.
- Faith extinguishes incoming lies.

Helmet of Salvation

- Guard the mind.
- Refuse shame God has forgiven.
- A protected mind leads to a protected life.

Sword of the Spirit: The Word of God

- Scripture must be spoken, not just stored.
- Jesus answered lies with "It is written."
- So do Kingdom Soldiers.

4. Daily Engagement Protocol

Morning

- Report for duty.
- Pray before consuming information

- Align with the Commander.

Word Intake

- Feed before fighting.
- Nourishment matters more than volume.
- Truth stored becomes ammunition.

Prayer

- Communication, not performance.
- Keeps you aligned with your assignment.
- Prevents fighting the wrong battles.

Awareness

- Stay alert, not anxious.
- Pay attention to peace lifting or remaining.
- Awareness is maturity, not paranoia.

5. Recognizing an Active Attack

You may be under spiritual pressure if you notice:

- Sudden confusion about truth you once held clearly.
- Increased condemnation or shame.
- Strong temptation to isolate.
- Loss of peace without obvious cause.
- Compulsion to abandon your post.
- Fatigue that is disproportionate to effort.

Do not panic.
Do not self-diagnose emotionally.

Return to truth, position, and prayer.

6. When You Get Hit

Every soldier does.
　　Immediate response:

1. Confess quickly.
2. Receive grace fully.
3. Reject shame completely.
4. Re-engage obedience immediately.

Falling is not defeat.
Staying down is.
A wounded soldier who gets up is still dangerous.

7. Holding Your Post

Every believer has an assignment.
　　Not every assignment is visible.
　　Faithfulness in obscurity is still greatness.
　　Ask daily:

"Lord, what is mine to hold today?"

Distraction is often more dangerous than direct attack.

8. Brotherhood and Reinforcement

Isolation weakens resistance.
　　Unity strengthens resolve.
　　Accountability keeps blind spots exposed.
　　If the enemy can separate you, he can wear you down.
　　Stay connected.

9. The Kingdom Soldier's Rule of Engagement

Do not fight people.
Do not abandon your post.
Do not negotiate with lies.
Do not operate disconnected from the Commander.
Do not confuse emotion with truth.
Fight spiritually.
Stand faithfully.
Advance quietly and consistently.

10. Core Scriptures to Keep Loaded

- Ephesians 6:10–18
- 2 Corinthians 10:3–5
- Colossians 2:15
- James 4:7
- 1 Peter 5:8–9
- Romans 8:1
- Joshua 1:8

Know where they are.
Return to them often.

FINAL REMINDER

Spiritual warfare is not dramatic most of the time.
It is daily.
It is quiet.
It is won through faithfulness.
Stand your ground.
Hold your post.
Listen for the Commander's voice.

And remember:
You are not fighting alone.
You are not under-equipped.
You are not late to the battle.
You are a Kingdom Soldier.

KINGDOM ASSIGNMENT
DISCOVERY GUIDE
APPENDIX C

This guide is not about finding a title.

It is about recognizing your post.

Assignments in the Kingdom are not chosen. They are received.

They are discerned through obedience, faithfulness, and attention to where God has already placed you.

Use this guide prayerfully. Move slowly. Write honestly.

SECTION 1: REAFFIRM YOUR POSITION

Before asking what you are called to do, you must remember who you are.

Speak these statements out loud or in writing.

- I belong to God. I am not self-directed.
- I am under authority before I exercise authority.
- I am part of an army, not a free agent.
- My value is not measured by visibility or applause.
- Obedience matters more than outcome.

If you resist any of these statements, pause here.

Assignment clarity does not come to those still negotiating surrender.

Prayer:

Lord, I submit again to Your authority. I am available for Your purposes, not my preferences.

SECTION 2: IDENTIFY YOUR CURRENT POST

Most believers miss their assignment because they are looking ahead instead of around.

Answer honestly.

1. Where has God already placed responsibility in my life?

- Family
- Marriage
- Children
- Workplace
- Church
- Community
- A specific person or burden

2. What has God entrusted to me that would be harmed if I walked away?

Your assignment is often revealed by what would suffer if you abandoned it.

3. What am I currently doing faithfully, even if no one notices?

Consider this prayerfully.

Write your answer:

My current post appears to be ________________________________.

SECTION 3: DISCERN THE BURDEN GOD HAS GIVEN YOU

Kingdom assignments are often revealed through holy burden, not preference.

Reflect carefully.

- What injustice, need, or brokenness consistently stirs my heart?
- What do I notice that others seem to overlook?
- What problems do I pray about without being prompted?
- What issues make it hard for me to remain passive?

Do not confuse burden with anger alone.

Godly burden moves you toward intercession and action, not cynicism.

Write:

The burden God has placed on my heart is ______________.

SECTION 4: INVENTORY WHAT GOD HAS PLACED IN YOUR HANDS

God rarely assigns without equipping.
Answer without false humility.

1. What skills, abilities, or gifts do I possess?
2. What life experiences has God used to shape me?
3. What pain or valleys have formed wisdom in me?
4. What do others consistently ask me for help with?

Your scars often reveal your assignment.

Write:

God has equipped me through ________________________________.

SECTION 5: CLARIFY THE SCOPE OF YOUR ASSIGNMENT

Not every assignment is permanent.
Not every assignment is expansive.
Ask these questions:

- Is this assignment for a season or a lifetime?
- Is it focused on one person, a group, or a place?
- Is God calling me to build, guard, heal, teach, or restore?

Avoid ambition here. Seek accuracy.

Write:

The scope of my assignment seems to be ______________________.

SECTION 6: TEST FOR ALIGNMENT AND PEACE

God does not lead through confusion.
    Check alignment in three areas:

1. Scripture

Does this assignment violate or contradict God's Word?

2. Peace

Does peace remain when I consider stepping forward in obedience?

3. Confirmation

Has God affirmed this direction through prayer, counsel, or circumstance?

Peace does not mean ease.
    It means settled alignment beneath difficulty.

Write:

When I submit this assignment to God, I sense ______________.

SECTION 7: IDENTIFY THREATS TO YOUR ASSIGNMENT

The enemy targets assignments through predictable tactics.
Circle any that apply:

- Distraction
- Fear of inadequacy
- Comparison
- Isolation
- Busyness
- Discouragement
- Shame from past failure

Awareness is protection.

Write:

The primary threats to my assignment are ________________.

SECTION 8: COMMIT TO FAITHFUL ACTION

Assignments are clarified through movement, not waiting.
Answer this:
What is one obedient step I can take in the next seven days?
Not the whole mission.
Just the next faithful step.

Write:

This week, obedience looks like ____________________________.

SECTION 9: COVENANT STATEMENT

Read this aloud. Then sign it.

> *I acknowledge that I have been entrusted with a Kingdom assignment.*
> *I commit to hold my post faithfully, whether seen or unseen.*
> *I will resist distraction, refuse passivity, and obey promptly.*
> *I place outcomes in God's hands and offer Him my faithfulness.*

Signed: _______________________

Date: _______________________

FINAL INSTRUCTION

Do not wait to feel qualified.

Do not wait for clarity to become perfect.

Do not wait for permission from people God did not appoint.

Assignments are confirmed in obedience.

Hold your post.

Stand your ground.

Advance faithfully.

And when you learn to stand, train another.

Your soldier is waiting.

ABOUT THE AUTHOR

Richard Robinson is a Kingdom-minded Christian teacher and writer devoted to equipping believers to understand their identity, authority, and assignment in Christ. He teaches with the conviction that every believer's calling matters and that no assignment in God's Kingdom is insignificant, hidden, or disposable.

Through Scripture-centered teaching and practical spiritual insight, Richard presents the Christian life as a call to disciplined, obedient, and courageous Kingdom living. His work challenges believers to move beyond passive Christianity and step fully into purposeful service under the authority of Christ, standing firm in faith and ready for the work God has entrusted to them.

Richard's writing consistently emphasizes spiritual readiness, trust in God, and faithfulness in daily obedience. *Kingdom Soldiers* was written to inspire Christians from every walk of life to recognize their role in God's Kingdom and to advance with clarity, conviction, and confidence. He believes the Kingdom advances through ordinary faithfulness lived consistently, and that disciples are called to make disciples.

Richard lives in Normal, Illinois, with his wife of 32 years, Linda "Tuey." They have four adult children, Richard Isaac, Chamara, Ramone, and Xavier, and five grandchildren.

ACKNOWLEDGMENTS

I would like to thank my wife Tuey and my children, who were so instrumental in the writing of this book:

Richard Isaac, Chamara, Ramone, and Xavier.

I would also like to thank a few Kingdom Soldiers whose lives touched so many along their journeys:

Carmen, my first wife, who helped to shape me into the man that I am.

Denzil, Tuey's first husband, a pillar of the faith and my best friend.

Clarice Ray, my mom, a strong, spirited woman who was "Aunt Bouquet" to so many.

Evangelist Floyd Brown, my spiritual father.

JoAnna Caldwell, my spiritual mom, a fighter for the underdog.

Fannie Washington, Carmen's mother, a prayer warrior.

Bishop Harold & Mattie P. Dawson, for the years of caring and teaching fundamental biblical truths.

Pastor Ed and Beth Herald and the Victory Church family.

Pastor Dana and Jackie Dunson and the Hallelujah Worship Church family.

Pastor Polly Pulley and the Spirit of Faith Church family.

Hilda, Evelyn, Jan, and Angela, my dear sisters that I cherish.

Pastor William Robinson, Pastor Joseph Brown, Pastor Bob Smart, Minister Donna Powell, and Minister and Lilly Meiner.

Lastly, my writing community: Jeff, Angie, Abigail, Sarah, Doc, Derek, Roxanne...

Thank you all.

ADVANCE HIS KINGDOM, SOLDIER...ADVANCE!

www.ingramcontent.com/pod-product-compliance
Lightning Source LLC
Chambersburg PA
CBHW051506030726
47592CB00006B/2130